D1301816

OIL PRICES AND TRADE DEFICITS

Oil Prices and Trade Deficits

U.S. Conflicts with Japan and West Germany

David Gisselquist

PRAEGER

PRAEGER SPECIAL STUDIES • PRAEGER SCIENTIFIC

Library of Congress Cataloging in Publication Data

Gisselquist, David.
    Oil prices and trade deficits.

    Includes bibliographical references.
    1. Petroleum products--Prices. 2. Balance of trade--
United States. 3. United States--Foreign economic
relations--Germany, West. 4. United States--Foreign
economic relations--Japan. I. Title.
HD9560.4.G57   382.1'7'0973   79-20632
ISBN 0-03-052381-8

Published in 1979 by Praeger Publishers
A Division of Holt, Rinehart and Winston/CBS, Inc.
383 Madison Avenue, New York, New York 10017 U.S.A.

© 1979 by Praeger Publishers

9 038 987654321

Printed in the United States of America

ACKNOWLEDGEMENTS

This book was written with the assistance and support of numerous people. Some of the ideas were first developed with Leonard Rapping while discussing international economic issues of the 1970s. Irwin Zuckerman shared in the earliest attempts to organize the ideas for the book and read early drafts of several chapters. Betsy Schmidt provided invaluable help in research; Bill Goodfellow shared his library. Jim Morrell read early drafts, and provided criticism and encouragement. Where ideas impinged on their areas of expertise, Wendy Takacs and Max Holland provided valuable guidance. The manuscript was prepared for the publisher with the assistance of Mary Speck. Joanne Gisselquist proofread the final draft. Finally, thanks are due the editors at Praeger Publishers who worked with a difficult manuscript and an author over 10,000 miles away.

CONTENTS

LIST OF TABLES AND FIGURE

OIL PRICES AND
TRADE DEFICITS

1

TRILATERALISM ON THE SKIDS

Economic and strategic interests of the United States lead logically to U.S. support for high world oil prices. The proposition that the United States favors high world oil prices leads in turn to a reinterpretation of the serious economic disagreements that have divided Western Europe, the United States, and Japan in the 1970s. This book is an attempt to identify and explain U.S. government support for the oil cartel and from such a vantage point to reinterpret international economic difficulties of the 1970s.

Economic size largely determines which nations are crucial to the maintenance of stability in international economic matters; aside from the Soviet Union, which is only partially integrated into world trade patterns, the United States, Japan, and West Germany are the three largest nations in terms of both GNP and total exports. In recent years, those economic conflicts that have developed between the United States, Japan, and West Germany have been the most threatening to international economic order.

In some sense, these conflicts have their basis in World Wars I and II. Both Japan and Germany, as losers in war, lost colonies and oil concessions; the victors, including France, England, and the United States, kept their colonies and their foreign investments. At present, the heavy dependence of Japan and West Germany on increasingly vulnerable supplies of foreign resources impels them to seek independent international economic strength, but their quest for power through export promotion in the 1970s has met with the opposition of the United States.

In 1971 President Nixon formally initiated the modern era of economic conflict by presenting new U.S. international economic policies as unilateral demands rather than through the usual careful and circumspect pattern of conference and compromise. The oil-price increases of 1973 represent a major escalation in the tactics of economic confrontation and commercial aggression. Higher world prices for oil especially hurt resource-poor Japan and several industrialized Western European countries. Japan and West Germany have responded with aggressive programs to expand exports while imports have lagged. Despite their higher bills for oil imports, both Japan and West Germany have recorded large trade surpluses in the middle and late 1970s, while the United States has been faced with record deficits.

The seriousness of the developing conflict between the United States and other noncommunist industrial nations is not generally appreciated in the United States. Inability to understand the conflict is apparent in public confusion about world oil prices and the attitude of the U.S. government on high oil prices. Within the United States, much of the public believes that the United States is suffering from the oil crisis like all other industrial nations. But the facts speak otherwise: Western Europe and Japan are much more dependent on imported oil than is the United States. The relative complacency of the United States in the face of oil-price increases has not gone unnoticed in Japan and Western Europe. Naturally, the complacent response by the United States to oil-price increases makes it very difficult for Western Europe and Japan to exert on their own any pressure for lower prices. In the middle and late 1970s, their displeasure was expressed through export and import policies that forced the United States to negotiate with them on trade—and on the related matter of U.S. energy policies.

The disagreement between the "big three" over oil prices and other trade matters has already led to a serious world recession in 1975 as major market countries cut imports and recessed their economies at least in part to avoid going into debt to pay their higher oil bills. Although the major nations soon recovered from the 1975 recession, protectionism still looms as a major threat, for all nations are paying close attention to trade balances. Producer groups in major industrial nations are taking the opportunity offered by current concern with trade balances to urge quotas and tariffs to protect domestic jobs and profits. The recent public debates over steel import quotas demonstrated the alacrity with which tariffs and quotas can be accepted as solutions to U.S. economic problems. For other nations the situation is similar. But any general move toward protectionism in a world with multinational companies, export-oriented economies, and an international division of labor between developed and underdeveloped countries could create instability and a recession serious enough to have dangerous political consequences in many countries.

Whatever else happens, oil-price increases will necessarily accelerate the trend toward independence in world affairs for Western European nations and Japan as they struggle to build their own regions of stability within a world of disagreement. Although they have relied since World War II on the United States to provide supervision of markets and to maintain low prices for raw materials, the present conflict of interest is forcing realization that the United States can no longer be relied upon to serve the interests of Japan and of Western Europe. If West Germany or France, for example, could expand its influence in one or two oil-exporting countries, then its oil supply would be more secure. If Japan could extend its influence in Southeast Asia, then some of its primary product needs and parallel need for export markets could be satisfied in a protected environment. In future years, Third World countries will be increasingly wooed (or subverted, depending on one's point of view) by Japan and by several Western European nations, as well as by the United States and the Soviet Union. Deterioration in political and economic relationships between the major industrial countries has already occurred as a result of the oil crisis; further deterioration is a distinct possibility.

DIFFERENTIAL IMPACT OF THE ENERGY CRISIS

Immediately after the beginning of the oil embargo and the price increase of October 1973, the value of the U.S. dollar began to rise against the currencies of nearly all other industrial countries (Figure 1.1). The one exception, Canada, was self-sufficient in oil. In general, any increase in the value of the dollar indicates that people are willing to pay more for dollars, either as an investment or to buy U.S. goods for export. An increase in a short period of time in response to some change in circumstances, as occurred after the October oil-price increase, can only be explained as reflecting the judgment of people with money (international bankers, currency analysts in multinational corporations, central bankers, and so on) that the dollar should go up. Their judgment would have been based at least in part on the resource positions of the various countries.

In 1973, the United States provided over 80 percent of its energy from domestic sources, chiefly petroleum and natural gas. Japan in the same year provided only 10 percent of its own energy from domestic sources. Oil, which supplied 78 percent of Japan's energy needs, was over 99 percent imported, mostly from the Middle East. In the case of Japan, even most coal is imported: imports of coal in 1973 provided 12 percent of Japan's total energy needs against 4 percent provided by domestically mined coal. For West Germany, imports of oil accounted for 52 percent of its total energy needs; imports of natural gas added 4 percent to its dependence on external energy supplies. Overall, West Germany in 1973

FIGURE 1.1

Exchange Rates against the Dollar

(percentage deviations from dollar Smithsonian parities of December 1971;
weekly averages of daily figures in U.S. dollars per unit)

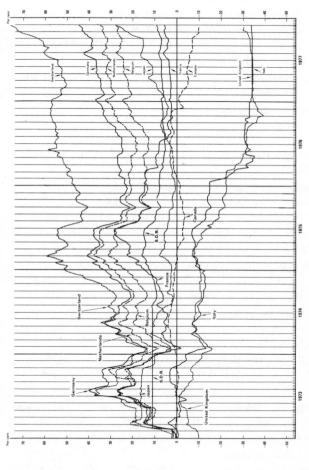

Note: S.D.R. is Special Drawing Rights.
Source: Organization for Economic Cooperation and Development (OECD), Economic Outlook 22 (Paris; OECD, December 1977), p. 132. Reprinted by permission.

4

depended on imports for 56 percent of its total energy consumption. For Western Europe as a whole, imports of oil alone provided over 60 percent of total energy needs.[1] Clearly, among the major non-communist industrial countries, the United States was in the best shape with domestic supplies of energy (Table 1.1).

U.S. domestic production of oil in 1973 (averaging 9.2 million barrels per day) exceeded total oil consumption in West Germany (2.7 million barrels per day) and Japan (5.0 million barrels per day) combined.[2] That the United States also imported over a third of its oil consumption needs in 1973 reflects the very high rate of energy use in the United States.

Turning from oil and natural gas to alternate sources of energy, the U.S. advantage over other industrialized market economies is even greater. In both coal and uranium, the United States has been a net exporter and should become more important as an exporter if other nations try to reduce their dependence on oil. U.S. reserves and reserves of other nations of both coal and uranium are shown in Table 1.2.

The degree of energy autarky for each country is roughly reflected in domestic energy prices. Energy prices in Japan and West Germany are in many cases more than double those in the United States. To some extent, the higher prices merely reflect higher production and transportation costs, but to a significant degree energy prices are determined by government policy. Prices of oil products are shown in Table 1.3. For natural gas and coal, the second and third most important fuels in the United States, Japan, and West Germany, prices in the United States averaged less than half those of West Germany and Japan in 1975.[3] Despite the energy crisis, the price of gasoline in the United States from 1975 through 1978 was lower in real terms (discounting for inflation) than when President Kennedy was elected (see Table 1.4). Clearly, the U.S. economy has been in a privileged position throughout the energy crisis.

At this point, the expected effect of the oil crisis on industrial activities in Japan, Western Europe, and the United States should be clear: since the United States would be able to rely on domestic sources of energy—as one of the three largest oil producers in the world (along with the Soviet Union and Saudi Arabia) and as the owner of the largest reserves of coal and uranium in the world—U.S. energy prices would be able to stay low, giving U.S. producers a decided cost advantage over producers in all other major industrialized market economies (except for Canada).

TABLE 1.1

Energy Dependence of the Three Major Noncommunist Industrial Countries, 1973
(percent total energy consumption)

	United States	Japan	West Germany
Oil			
Total	47	78	55
Domestic	30	a	3
Foreign	17	77	52
Coal and lignite			
Total	18	16	31
Domestic	18	4	31
Foreign	b	12	b
Natural gas			
Total	30	2	10
Domestic	29	1	7
Foreign	1	1	4
Nuclear	1	1	1
All other	4	5	3
Totals			
Domestic	82	10	44
Foreign	18	90	56

[a]Negligible.

[b]Net exporter.

Sources: U.S. Department of Energy (DOE), Monthly Energy Review (Washington, D.C.: DOE, January 1978), pp. 8, 26, 30, 32, 46; Bundeswirtschaftministerium, Das Energieprogramm der Bundesregierung (September 26, 1973), in Horst Mendershausen, Coping with the Oil Crisis (Baltimore: Johns Hopkins Press for Resources for the Future, 1976), pp. 34, 90; Commodity Research Bureau, 1978 Commodity Year Book (New York: Commodity Research Bureau, 1978), p. 168; Sogo Enerugii Tokei, edited by Agency of Natural Resources and Energy Directorate, General Secretariat, Tokyo, 1974, pp. 176-89, in Yuan-li Wu, Japan's Search for Oil (Stanford: Hoover Institution Press, 1977), p. 21.

TABLE 1.2

Reserves of Coal and Uranium for Selected Countries

	Reserve Base of Coal (billions short tons)	Reserves of Uranium and Uranium Oxide (U_3O_8) @ ($30/pound) (short tons)
United States	438	680,000
Japan	1	not a major producer
West Germany	109	not a major producer
Canada	16	225,000
France	1	72,000
India	26	not a major producer
Republic of South Africa	36	259,000
United Kingdom	111	not a major producer
Gabon	not a major producer	26,000
Niger	not a major producer	65,000
Namibia	not a major producer	100,000
Other market economies	6	610,000
Central market economies	330	moderate
World total	1,185	2,500,000

Sources: U.S. Department of Interior, Bureau of Mines, Mineral Commodity Summaries 1978 (Washington, D.C.: Government Printing Office, 1978), pp. 41, 183; K. P. Wang and staff, Bureau of Mines, U.S. Department of Interior, Far East and South Asia (Washington, D.C.: Government Printing Office, 1977), p. 45.

TABLE 1.3

Taxes and Duties on Important Petroleum Products
(data for July 31, 1976; all prices in
cents unless % is indicated)

	Retail Price*	Duty*	Tax*
France			
Regular	140.0	no duty	54.8%
Premium	150.8	no duty	53.9%
Distillate fuel oil	96.9	no duty	49.2%
Bunker "C" fuel oil	1,306.3	no duty	no tax
West Germany (Bonn)			
Regular	138.6	6%	65.6¢ + 11%
Premium	147.5	6%	65.6¢ + 11%
Distillate fuel oil	91.7	6%	31.7¢ + 11%
Bunker "C" fuel oil	1,369.2	3.5%	88.2¢ + 11%
Japan (Tokyo)			
Regular	136.1	2.7	56.7
Premium	151.2	2.7	56.7
Distillate fuel oil	86.9	2.3	26.5
Bunker "C" fuel oil	1,425.5	34.9	no tax
United States (New York)			
Regular	63.9	1.3	13.0
Premium	67.9	1.3	13.0
Distillate fuel oil	61.9	not available	13.0
Bunker "C" fuel oil	1,248.0	no duty	no tax
United States (San Francisco)			
Regular	57.5	1.3	11.0
Premium	61.5	1.3	11.0
Distillate fuel oil	55.5	not available	11.0
Bunker "C" fuel oil	1,000.0	no duty	no tax

*U.S. cents per U.S. gallon except for bunker "C" fuel oil which is U.S. cents per 42-gallon barrel.

Source: U.S. Department of the Interior, Bureau of Mines, International Petroleum Annual, 1975 (Washington, D.C.: Government Printing Office, 1977), pp. 30-36.

TABLE 1.4

U.S. Price of Gasoline, 1960–76
(average retail price per gallon of regular gasoline,
in cents based on actual and constant 1975 dollars)

	Actual	Constant
1960	31.1	57.6
1961	30.8	56.6
1962	30.6	55.2
1963	30.4	54.0
1964	30.4	53.2
1965	31.2	53.4
1966	32.1	53.2
1967	33.2	53.5
1968	33.7	51.9
1969	34.8	51.1
1970	35.7	49.7
1971	36.4	48.2
1972	36.1	45.9
1973	38.8	46.7
1974	52.8	57.7
1975	56.2	56.2
1976	58.7	55.8

Source: Federal Energy Administration (FEA), Energy in Focus: Basic Data (Washington, D.C.: FEA, 1977), p. 11.

AFTER THE PRICE RISE: INTENSIFIED
CONFLICT OVER TRADE

The direct effects of the oil-price increase did bear out the expectations: in general, those nations without substantial supplies of domestic energy experienced higher import bills for oil, higher rates of inflation, and more serious cutbacks in oil consumption than did the United States. Nevertheless, the United States found itself, in the late 1970s, with massive trade deficits and a seriously weakening dollar. For their part, both Japan and West Germany claimed to be having problems with inflation and sluggish domestic demand. Many other nations were arguing or had argued that they had special economic problems related to their oil-import bills.

The key to all of these problems is that along with the oil-price increases of the 1970s—and to some degree because of the price increases—has come intensified economic conflict among the major market economies. The arena of conflict is international trade, in which the current account surpluses or deficits of the various nations are the best indicators of the course of events.

At this point it is necessary to explain a basic concept in international economics: the current-account balance. A country acquires foreign exchange through export sales of merchandise to nonresidents, sales of services to nonresidents (for example, tourist services), and receipt of gifts from nonresidents (for example, foreign aid). Current foreign expenditures of a country are similarly made up of imports of goods and services and gifts to foreigners. The sum of all these items is the current-account balance. In 1977, for example, the United States purchased from the rest of the world $31 billion more in goods than were sold to the rest of the world. If we figure in services (including large profits of foreign investments) and international gifts (foreign aid), we get a deficit on current account of $15 billion: total sales of U.S. goods and services to and grants received from the rest of the world came to $15 billion less than the total of goods and services that the U.S. purchased from and grants given to the rest of the world. This indicates, in general, an increase in net U.S. debt to foreigners.

Since the late 1960s the major trading nations in the world—the United States, Japan, and West Germany—have been struggling with each other for current-account surpluses. For Japan and West Germany, the drive for current-account surpluses represents a desire to expand their economic power in the world, both through foreign investment and through greater leverage in world financial matters. Current-account surpluses provide for an increase in foreign assets by the surplus nation. A current-account surplus also represents success with exports. The United States, Japan, and West Germany have each been keen to expand their industrial exports so as to permit industrial development to proceed as quickly as possible, to promote full employment and high profits, and to increase national power at the expense of other industrial nations.

Intense competition for world market shares and current-account surpluses led in 1971 to a breakdown of agreement on fixed exchange rates between the major industrial nations: each nation wanted its currency to be cheap so that its goods would be cheap in world markets, giving it a competitive advantage against other industrial countries. The struggle over current-account surpluses has continued since 1971.

A particularly difficult episode occurred after the 1973 oil-price increases, when large oil revenues for the OPEC states complicated the struggle between the "big three." In 1974, OPEC states together had a current-account surplus over $60 billion. Not until 1977 did the OPEC surplus dip below $30 billion. By comparison, aggregate current-account surpluses for all surplus nations in the world averaged just $15 billion in the years to 1973. The large OPEC current-account surpluses after 1973—representing exports unmatched by imports—meant that other nations would have to run current-account deficits—representing imports unmatched by exports. The reasonable solution would have been for the United States, Japan, and West Germany to share some of the balancing deficits. Instead, they continued to fight for surpluses, pushing deficits onto others—such as England and Italy (which soon found it necessary to undertake vigorous and painful programs to correct their large current-account deficits) and Brazil, South Korea, and Mexico (which borrowed large amounts from foreign banks to keep imports coming in despite high import prices and lower than expected export sales).

By 1976, the United States had begun to reduce its current-account surplus and increase its imports in order to help other nations reduce their deficits. But at that point, Japan was in the process of a drive for new record current-account surpluses, and West Germany continued with its consistent large surpluses. The surpluses by Japan and West Germany continued to make it difficult for other nations to avoid large, unwanted deficits. Accordingly, the United States made several proposals designed to enlist the cooperation of Japan and West Germany in sharing the balancing deficits necessary to match OPEC surpluses.

The first proposal, known as the "locomotive" solution, urged Japan and West Germany to follow the U.S. locomotive, pulling the nations of the world out of the 1975 recession with a policy of high growth and increased imports to support economic expansion elsewhere in the world. U.S. government negotiators were unable to enlist West German and Japanese cooperation in the locomotive solution. Soon the nomenclature changed from locomotive to "convoy" solution—essentially the same solution under a new name. U.S. negotiators were no more successful with the new name than they had been with the old one.

Both the locomotive and the convoy solutions proposed that the big three should grow so as to suck in more imports and thereby transfer deficits from others to themselves. Although both the locomotive and the convoy solutions seem to be based on higher rates of economic growth in Japan and West Germany, this is not entirely correct. By growth, U.S. negotiators meant an increase in imports and maybe even a decrease in exports. If the governments of Japan and West Germany would "reflate" or "pump up" their economies, as the argument goes, consumers and businesses would buy more goods, more imports, and maybe even some goods which would otherwise be exported. What the United States was pushing for was not wealthier Japanese and West Germans, but rather a reduction in the current-account surpluses of Japan and West Germany. For U.S. officials to phrase their suggestions in terms of higher growth was merely a politeness necessary to avoid exciting Japanese and West German sensitivities. What U.S. negotiators wanted to say and what they were implying was, "Import more and export less."

The resistance of Japan and West Germany to the locomotive and convoy solutions was similarly couched in obfuscation. Japanese and West German negotiators argued that inflation remained a threat in their economies. They pleaded an inability to do anything in the short run. What they were saying was, "No, we will keep our surpluses."

The struggle at this point seems completely one-sided: the U.S. position that Japanese and West German surpluses were threats to world economic stability was so elementary and obvious that it had to be understood by West German and Japanese negotiators, yet there was no agreement. The deficits to offset OPEC surpluses should have gone to Japan and to West Germany as well as to the United States by any standard economic logic. To give the deficits to the rest of the world threatened recession in the weaker industrial countries (such as England and Italy) and also led to accelerated debt buildup in Third World nations with large deficits. The U.S. negotiators were absolutely right in pushing for reduction of the Japanese and West German surpluses. Then why did Japanese and West German negotiators resist?

This line of argument leads to some speculative suspicions: Japanese and West German policy makers may have been deliberately running the surpluses in full knowledge of the possible consequences. At least in part, the surpluses may have been intended as threats to bring the United States to the bargaining table. Certainly, one consequence of the surpluses was a vigorous attempt by the United States to negotiate for their elimination. The United States appointed a high-powered trade negotiator, Ambassador Robert Strauss, who reported directly to the president, to carry on negotiations with Western Europe and Japan over surpluses and other matters of trade policy.

Negotiations to reduce Japanese and West German current-account surpluses were singularly unsuccessful through 1978 despite the simplicity, accuracy, and logic of the U.S. position and of its proposed solution to the world economic crisis. It is significant, however, in the light of continued intransigence by West

Germany and Japan over their continued current-account surpluses that they brought the matter of the U.S. energy program—or the lack of one—into the discussions. From the published "Joint Statement by Minister Ushiba and Ambassador Strauss" following two days of talks in January 1978, we can clearly see that U.S. concern about Japan's current-account surpluses was met with Japanese criticism of the U.S. energy "nonprogram."

> Japan has undertaken steps aimed at achieving a marked diminution of its current account surplus. The Minister added that . . . Japan's current account surplus would be considerably reduced through the expansion of domestic demand, the effect of yen appreciation in recent months, and a series of new measures for improving the access of foreign goods to the Japanese market . . . all reasonable efforts would be continued with a view to further reducing Japan's current account surplus, aiming at equilibrium, with deficit accepted if it should occur.
>
> The United States stated its intention to improve its balance of payments position by such measures as reducing its dependence on imported oil and increasing its exports, thereby improving the underlying conditions upon which the value of the dollar fundamentally depends. The Ambassador expressed confidence that in the next ninety days an effective energy program would be enacted by the Congress.[4]

Although the problem of balancing OPEC surpluses with deficits elsewhere was essentially solved by 1978 with a drop in OPEC surpluses to about $11 billion, continuing large current-account surpluses by Japan and smaller ones by West Germany left the United States with substantial deficits in 1977 and 1978. Along with these developments, the locomotive and convoy solutions gave way to "convergence," a proposal which is again expressed in terms of growth rates (that is, that West Germany and Japan should grow faster and the United States should grow slower), but which is again an attempt to persuade Japan and West Germany to reduce their current-account surpluses so as to help the United States get out of deficit. Despite the drop in OPEC current-account surpluses, U.S. negotiators continue to meet Japanese and West German representatives to discuss U.S. energy policies and the surpluses of Japan and West Germany. With the reduction of OPEC surpluses, however, the pressure of unwanted deficits on other nations has been reduced, giving the United States more room to maneuver in attempting to get rid of its own deficits without having to worry so much about the effect of such a policy on other nations.

GROUNDS FOR SUSPICION: THE UNITED STATES AND HIGH WORLD OIL PRICES

Just as U.S. negotiators have been concerned with Japan's and West Germany's trade surpluses and not with the welfare of the Japanese and West German people in advocating a policy of high growth for the two nations, so also may we suppose that Japanese and West European negotiators have been concerned with matters other than the U.S. energy bill when they have advocated enactment of a U.S. energy program. The United States is implicated in the world oil crisis in several ways, on both the demand and the supply sides of the market. Overall U.S. imports of oil increased from an average of around 20 percent of U.S. oil consumption in the 1960s to 48 percent of U.S. oil consumption in 1977.[5] By the end of 1977, U.S. oil imports as a share of total OPEC production came to 28 percent, up from about 15 percent in 1970.[6] The United States, through wasteful habits of energy use, was forced to go to foreign producers and especially to the Middle East for more oil when its domestic supplies and traditional foreign suppliers (such as Venezuela) not only were outrun by growing U.S. demand but also began to run low.

The large size of recent U.S. imports of oil has not gone unnoticed in other countries. The use of oil and energy in the United States is profligate by the standards of any other oil-importing country in the world; there is ample scope for conservation cutbacks in energy use. Moreover, the United States is rich in alternatives to oil; an energy policy to replace imported oil with coal or shale oil, both of which are abundant, could be expected to have some effect on U.S. import requirements. But through 1978, the United States has neither conserved nor switched to domestic fuels fast enough to restrain its large oil purchases in world markets. Surely, there is much more that the United States could have done to reduce its support as a major importer for the high oil prices that have reigned in world markets since 1973.

The United States is also implicated on the production side of the market. Five of the "Seven Sisters," oil company giants that dominate the industry throughout the world, are U.S. companies. These companies reaped great profits from the 1973-74 price increases, both in their domestic production and in their international business as they shared the higher oil prices with the producer governments. In the price increases of 1973 there was more for the companies as well as the OPEC countries. As the home country of most of the major companies in international oil, the United States understandably has at times designed its foreign policy to benefit U.S. oil companies; and that may be part of the story of 1973 as well.

The influence and intended influence of the U.S. government on oil prices in the 1970s does not need to be proven beyond any doubt for West Germany and Japan to recognize a conflict with the United States over oil prices. In international affairs, suspicions and plausible interpretations are the only proofs available in many cases. If U.S. actions have in fact supported higher oil prices, and if motives exist which would lead the United States to support higher oil prices, then there is sufficient cause for West Germany and Japan to take offense at the U.S. position and to attempt to nudge U.S. policy toward opposition to high oil prices.

The common U.S. refrain has been that OPEC governments were responsible, acting in total opposition to U.S. wishes, and even making life more difficult for the oil companies. From such a view, the situation is totally out of control, but we forget thereby the U.S. impact on world oil markets through its vastly increased import demand for oil.

A standard radical interpretation would have it that the U.S. oil companies played a large part in the oil-price increases. In such a scenario, the U.S. government is either the hostage of the oil companies against the interests of nearly every other group in the United States or else is simply on the sidelines, ineffective and unaware.

A full and simple conspiracy theory would have the U.S. government support the oil-price increase in order to strengthen the position of U.S. companies in the oil-producing countries, to slow down economic growth in Western Europe and Japan, to stabilize and to strengthen key Middle East allies, and to increase the wealth and profits of the U.S. oil industry at the expense of other countries around the world.

The kindest thing which can be said about U.S. actions through the oil-price increases of 1973 and later is that the U.S. government helplessly supported the oil-price increase through its oil companies and its oil imports, that the United States was hurt less than its major industrial rivals, but that good intentions ruled throughout. Nevertheless, after five years of higher world oil prices through 1978, U.S. inability to design an energy program that would significantly restrain its oil imports seems as willful a violation of the legitimate interests of Japan and West Germany as their continued current-account surpluses have been a violation of what the United States sees as the proper world order.

PLAN OF THE BOOK

Since the oil-price increases of 1973, much of the discussion in the United States about oil and energy has been sidetracked into condemnations of OPEC, speculation about new discoveries of oil, and so forth. But one important issue has been passed over: the oil price increase has placed the United States as a wasteful consumer and major producer of oil in opposition to the resource-poor but economically powerful countries of Japan and West Germany. At present the conflict is most apparent in disagreements over trade policies and over the foreign-exchange value of various currencies. Although the existence of disagreements with Western Europe and Japan over trade policies and currency values is widely recognized in the United States, the relationship of oil prices to other economic conflicts is not appreciated. Energy is one of the key economic issues between the United States, Western Europe, and Japan; without explicit recognition of such a conflict, discussions about energy in the United States have often been misleading. Accordingly, this book focuses on the relationship between oil-price increases and economic conflicts between the big three.

Chapter 2 provides a historical background for the current conflict. Economic growth in West Germany and Japan was encouraged by the United States as a geopolitical tactic after World War II: West Germany and Japan, though former enemies, were quickly rehabilitated as allies against the Soviet Union. Economic growth in both countries under U.S. guidance may also be seen as part of a plan to build a system of free trade among market economies, including as many countries as possible. As they were past and future industrial powers, it was only reasonable that Japan and West Germany be built into the system as well. Thus, the United States favored economic growth in Japan and West Germany through the 1950s and most of the 1960s.

By the late 1960s, however, increasing competition from the mature industrial countries of Japan and West Germany led the U.S. government to switch its policies from aid and support to opposition. The United States, instead of seeing its self-interest served by further economic advance for Japan and West Germany, began to see difficulties for itself in their economic success. President Nixon's 1971 efforts to reduce the value of the U.S. dollar relative to the mark and the yen were designed in a spirit of nationalistic self-interest against the interests of Japan and West Germany. Presumably, the United States in the early 1970s would have been interested as well in other policies to slow down the industrial advance of its rivals.

Chapter 3 deals with the role of the U.S. government in the world oil industry. In the twentieth century, and especially since World War II, the U.S. government has consistently worked through private, U.S. oil companies to extend and maintain its influence over the world oil industry. The oil-price increases of 1973 followed

several years of intensive secret discussions between the oil companies, home governments of the oil companies, and the governments of the oil-exporting countries. Throughout the period, the
U.S. government took several actions which look suspicious for
their impact in favor of higher oil prices. Significantly, a motive
for the U.S. government to support higher oil prices in the 1970s—
though not before—was supplied by its emerging sense of competition and conflict with West Germany and Japan, both of which are
much more dependent on foreign sources of oil and have much less
control over those foreign sources than does the United States.

Chapter 4 deals with the continuing post-1973 struggle for
current-account surpluses between the big three. One aspect of the
struggle from 1974-77 was that the large surpluses of OPEC made
large balancing deficits inevitable for the rest of the world. Since
the big three continued to struggle for surpluses, others were left
with deficits. For many nations, the large deficits they experienced
in 1974-77 were difficult to bear, affecting domestic employment
and necessitating large volumes of new foreign borrowing. Continued current-account surpluses by West Germany throughout the
post-1973 period and by Japan from 1976 appear to have been intended at least in part to pressure the United States on oil imports
and on world oil prices.

Although the global problem of balancing OPEC deficits was
solved by 1978 with the shrinkage of OPEC surpluses to an estimated $11 billion, continuing current-account surpluses for Japan
and West Germany were largely responsible for U.S. deficits in
1977-78. With their trade policies and in international negotiations,
Japan and West Germany continue to pressure the United States to
do something about its large oil-import bill and its support for high
world oil prices. Nevertheless, the shrinkage of OPEC surpluses
represented the success of a policy of high and higher oil prices,
and appeared to be bringing to a close one skirmish in the struggle
between the big three for world economic power.

Chapter 5 deals with foreign investment of surplus oil revenues by OPEC states and the increased level of international borrowing by deficit nations, especially during the 1974-77 period.
The United States has played the role of financial intermediary,
accepting OPEC investments on the one hand and making loans to
deficit nations on the other. Although the burden of debt for Third
World nations in general, and for most of the major debtors in
particular, actually declined during 1974-76 through the effect of
inflation in shrinking previous debt burdens, the size of current-
account deficits during these years, along with the proportionately
large role of private banks in providing loans to finance current-
account deficits, led to widespread worry about the long-term

security of the financial system. The United States, whose large
private banks provided much of the service of intermediation between OPEC saving nations and Third World borrowing nations was
particularly concerned. U.S. worries led to increases in the lending power of the International Monetary Fund, to enable that institution to better back up the banks, should their loans to any government become questionable.

Although the acute debt problems passed by 1976-77 with
the reduction of deficits for many non-oil, less developed countries,
the dangers involved in Third World governments' continuing to
borrow on a large scale from foreign private banks appears to be
a continuing worry. In the long run the role of the United States
and of U.S. banks as financial intermediaries will probably have to
be restrained in deference to the expansion of West German and
Japanese economic power.

Chapter 6 concludes with some speculation about future trade
and currency blocs, great-power relations, the future of the oil
cartel, and the case for an energy-conservation program in the
United States.

NOTES

1. Stockholm International Peace Research Institute, Oil and
Security (New York: Humanities Press, 1974), p. 14.
2. Federal Energy Administration, Energy in Focus: Basic
Data (Washington, D.C.: FEA, 1977), p. 5; U.S. Department of
Energy, Monthly Energy Review (Washington, D.C.: DOE, 1978),
p. 86.
3. Workshop on Alternative Energy Strategies, Energy:
Global Prospects 1985-2000 (New York: McGraw-Hill, 1977), p. 87.
4. "Joint Statement by Minister Ushiba and Ambassador
Strauss" (Washington, D.C.: U.S. Department of the Treasury,
January 1978), p. 2.
5. FEA, p. 6; DOE, p. 8. The figure for 1977 is for the
first 11 months.
6. FEA, p. 6; DOE, pp. 8, 88; John M. Blair, The Control
of Oil (New York: Random House, 1978), p. 100.

2

FROM WORLD WAR II TO 1973:
ECONOMIC GROWTH LEADS TO CONFLICT

> The Japanese are still fighting the war, but it is no
> longer a shooting war but an economic war. Their
> immediate aim is to try to dominate the Pacific, and
> after that, perhaps the whole world. [1]

The above quote, from an anonymous member of President
Nixon's cabinet in 1971, suggests a major change in attitude on the
part of U.S. leaders with respect to economic growth elsewhere in
the world. Although the speaker appears to have overstated the
competitive U.S. stance toward Japan, the words nevertheless reflect some of the thinking behind President Nixon's new economic
program of 1971 and behind basic U.S. policies toward Western
Europe and Japan throughout the 1970s. The new churlishness revealed in the quote represents a dramatic transformation in attitude
from the immediate post-World War II period when economic development anywhere outside the communist bloc was warmly welcomed
in Washington. Indeed, through the Marshall Plan in Western Europe
and through aid to Japan, the United States consciously promoted economic recovery and development in just those areas that have later
come to be seen as competitors and economic enemies in the United
States.
　　The key to the change in U.S. attitude and behavior toward
Western Europe and Japan is the change in relative economic size
that has occurred since World War II. At the end of the war the
United States was the leading industrial power of the world, having
emerged on the winning side without having suffered either occupation or air attacks. Although the entire developed world grew quickly after World War II, rates of growth varied from nation to nation.
In general, Japan and Western Europe were able to maintain higher
rates of economic growth throughout the period than was the United
States. By the 1970s, the cumulative effect of such higher rates of

growth had pushed the United States back into the pack, struggling for export markets and worried about its home markets against competition from Japan and Western Europe.

But there is another factor in the struggle between Japan, Western Europe, and the United States: U.S. military power is the basis for the alliance, and that is as true in the 1970s as it was in the 1940s. All of the noncommunist developed countries are heavily dependent on raw materials from Africa, Asia, and South America. With the dissolution of the empires of Europe the United States, through aid, foreign military bases, and occasional troop commitments, has carried more and more of the burden of keeping order in the Third World for the benefit of all developed countries. This process of replacing the nations of Europe and Japan in defense of former colonial areas has continued into the 1970s; for example, the new U.S. base on Diego Garcia in the Indian Ocean is designed to fill a power vacuum created in part by British withdrawal from Singapore in the 1970s.

And thus we have an asymmetry: the United States is declining in economic power relative to Japan and Western Europe, but such a decline has not affected its prominence as a military power. The decline in U.S. economic power creates tensions; under such circumstances there is a big temptation for the United States to use its diplomatic and military power for its own advantage in its economic conflicts with Western Europe and Japan. Furthermore, this temptation is of recent origin: roughly until the 1970s the United States identified its interests with economic growth in Western Europe and Japan so that any exercise of U.S. military and diplomatic power in favor of their economic expansion was consistent with U.S. self-interest and self-aggrandizement.

U.S. military preeminence has not changed. Presumably, the willingness of the United States to use its military and diplomatic power to serve its economic and strategic interests has not changed as well. But the conscious self-interest of the United States with respect to the continued, rapid economic expansion of Western Europe and Japan has changed. What effect such changes have or are thought to have on U.S. diplomatic and military policies around the world is a major factor complicating relations of the United States with its major allies in the 1970s and promising more problems in the 1980s.

U.S. STRATEGIC INTERESTS IN THE ECONOMIC RECOVERY OF WESTERN EUROPE AND JAPAN

In 1947 and 1948 the United States disengaged from its wartime alliance with the Soviet Union and embarked on a policy of "contain-

ment." Aside from its obvious military interpretation, the policy
of containment included U.S. commitment to the economic recovery
of Western Europe and Japan. Economic recovery of the war-
weakened countries to the east and west of the Soviet Union was designed to eliminate opportunities for political subversion and to
weave a pattern of stable and wealthy allies around the Soviet Union.[2]

In 1947 many of the countries of Western Europe were either
economically weak or politically vulnerable to indigenous leftist
movements. Although the Italian economy was recovering, the Communist Party's presence in parliament and in the labor unions was
feared in Washington. Prospects for French recovery under the
Monnet plan looked good, but again the Communist Party, with over
a quarter of the votes, raised concern in Washington. In Austria
and Germany, economic recovery was lagging. U.S. planners perceived a Soviet desire to exploit disintegration and weakness for
political gain. Consequently, when the Marshall Plan for U.S. assistance to Western Europe was designed and launched in 1947, the decision to go ahead with or without Soviet cooperation was a central
feature. Putting the Soviets on the sidelines amounted to claiming
the nations of Western Europe for the U.S. sphere.

As former enemies, Germany and Japan presented some problems to U.S. policy planners. Nevertheless, U.S. interests, as
expressed by George Kennan, chief of the State Department's Policy
Planning Staff during that crucial period, were clearly on the side of
industrial recovery and growth in Germany and Japan.

> As this tour d'horizon [late summer 1947] proceeded it
> became increasingly clear to me that the theaters of our
> greatest dangers, our greatest responsibilities, and our
> greatest possibilities at that moment were the two occu-
> pied areas of Western Germany and Japan. These
> places were the centers, respectively, of the two great-
> est industrial complexes of East and West. Their re-
> covery was essential to the restoration of stability in
> Europe and East Asia. It was essential, if any sort of
> a tolerable balance of power was to be established in
> the postwar world, that they be kept out of Communist
> hands and that their great resources be utilized to the
> full for constructive purposes.[3]

The inclusion of Germany and Japan in the U.S. plan for economic recovery involved some specific problems with the Soviet
Union. In the case of Germany, the Potsdam Conference between
the four powers (the United States, France, Great Britain, and the
USSR) had achieved agreement on various provisions relating to

coordinated four-power control of all four sections of occupied Germany. Soon after the close of the war, the agreement to cooperate began to look more and more like a constraint; in the words of George Kennan, the Potsdam agreement "caused us to lose nearly two years of valuable time."[4] The Soviet Union was insistent on using its influence to restrain the reemergence of a German challenge. The United States, more distant and more powerful, and also— with France and England—in control of a larger portion of Germany, saw the emergence of a strong Germany—or at least a strong portion of Germany under U.S. guidance—as a check on Soviet ambitions in Europe. An economically and politically strong Germany could be defended; it could be closely integrated into Western economic relations; its political institutions would be stable; and its industrial power would contribute to the strength of the noncommunist countries.

The U.S. decision to separate control of non-Soviet occupied Germany from the cooperative framework that had been set up at the end of the war was set in motion in 1947. A key element of separate administration was the currency reform of 1948 by which the U.S.-, French-, and British-occupied sectors of Germany were given a currency and a monetary policy that was separate from that of the Soviet sector. The currency reform was also one of the key elements in the German economic recovery. The pace of inflation was arrested, and that, combined with other changes in occupation policies, led to an annual rate of economic expansion of about 20 percent through 1950.[5]

The currency reform of June 1948 in Germany was "very largely of American design."[6] It was an essential precondition for the subsequent program of aided growth. In his history of German postwar economic recovery, Henry Wallich notes that

> Under the Potsdam Agreement the reform would have had to be carried through equally in all four zones. Protracted negotiations with the Russians, however, led nowhere. That the Western Allies preferred to let two years drag by rather than to proceed unilaterally attests to their realization that the splitting of the currency also meant the final splitting of Germany. When the currency reform was put through in June 1948, these unhappy expectations were fully realized, and the introduction of the new currency in West Berlin touched off the blockade of the city.[7]

The currency was split, Germany was split, and the Soviets retaliated with the Berlin blockade. Clearly, U.S. interests in the economic development of a U.S.-leaning portion of Germany were considered antagonistic to Russian interests.

A similar story can be told for Japan as well, except that, in the case of Japan, the U.S. use of nuclear weapons had precipitated the end of the war so quickly that the Soviet Union was not in a position to participate in the occupation of the main islands of Japan. The United States was in sole control of the occupation of Japan, although theoretically bound by the Potsdam agreement to cooperate with the Soviets in several matters until a peace treaty with Japan could be signed.

Initially, the U.S. occupation in Japan had punitive aspects. Efforts were expended on reform in several areas. Land reform was pushed in the countryside and trust-busting was pushed in industry. Japanese officials deemed responsible for aspects of the war effort were purged from positions of responsibility within the government or industry. These punitive aspects of the occupation inhibited economic recovery in the same manner that denazification in Germany hindered the recovery of Germany. In both nations the imposition of reparations payments—capital goods and raw materials— to the Allies was an additional impediment to recovery. But just as U.S. behavior toward Germany began to turn around with the emergence (or reemergence) of the Soviet Union as an enemy, U.S. policy toward Japan reversed as well.

In 1948 and 1949 various policy directives began to flow to General Douglas MacArthur from the State Department in Washington: economic recovery was to be sought at the expense of further reforms. The U.S. resolve on Japan was increased with the deterioration of the Nationalists in China; as Chiang Kai-shek got weaker and weaker in his battle with the Communists, U.S. concern about Japan grew.

Sometime in 1949 the decision was apparently taken in Washington to go ahead with a separate peace treaty and to conclude a security treaty with Japan at the same time. Japan was to be brought into alliance with the United States, U.S. troops were to remain stationed in Japan, and the recovery of Japanese industry was to be encouraged. Just as in the case of Germany, independent action by the United States in dealing with Japan was taken badly in the Kremlin. In Kennan's opinion, the peace treaty and security agreement with Japan "probably had an important bearing on the Soviet decision to unleash the attack in Korea."[8]

As part of its policy of containment, a policy of restrained belligerence toward the Soviet Union, the United States launched an aggressive program of aid for economic recovery in all of the important industrial countries outside of Soviet control. The policy to promote recovery took precedence over all punitive policies toward former enemies. The extension of U.S. influence that was intended in such policies—and that was perceived in Moscow—led to confrontations in Berlin and Korea. Nevertheless, U.S. policy intentions for France, Italy, Japan, Germany, and the other countries of Western Europe were achieved. Economic recovery succeeded, and leftist political movements were contained.

U.S. ECONOMIC INTERESTS IN THE RECOVERY OF WESTERN EUROPE AND JAPAN

A major goal of the United States in the postwar period was to establish a regime of free trade and ready access to markets for U.S. exports as well as U.S. access to raw-material imports.[9] To understand the significance of this drive one has to remember what happened to the United States during the depression years: in response to the decline in demand, worldwide protectionism to defend markets within the various colonial trading blocs had pushed U.S. exports out of much of the world. Sales of U.S. goods fell throughout Europe and its colonies, whose trade was controlled for the benefit of Great Britain, France, Portugal, and other European metropolitan countries.

One of the lessons of the depression for the United States was that the old colonial trading blocs had to be forced open if the U.S. economy was going to be able to sell and to buy as needed to accommodate its ability to grow and to produce. Bilateral trade relations and state control of economic affairs in pre-World War II Europe had helped to keep U.S. industry in stagnation throughout the 1930s until it was rescued by the war. The new postwar world was to be one of free access for U.S. exports throughout Europe and its former colonies.

In pursuit of its economic objective of avoiding a recurrence of the depression and of avoiding a return to Europe-centered trading blocs from which U.S. goods were excluded, the U.S. government used its economic and military power to open up the colonial empires, and European countries themselves, to U.S. trade. Lend-lease aid to Great Britain, for example, was made conditional upon British changes in certain empire policies to make it easier for U.S. businesses to sell to the colonies and to Great Britain itself.

Planners also feared that a postwar depression or recession could come with declining demand and unemployment as the war effort ended. The demand for U.S. production since the 1930s had been increased by the demand for war materials, bringing full employment and actually increasing consumer goods production during the war. But with the end of the war and a reduced demand for war goods, who would buy all the output that could be produced? The need for markets for U.S. industry coincided neatly with the need for goods in Europe and Japan. The United States could produce goods for export to help in the reconstruction of the war-damaged countries of Europe and Asia.

Theoretically, the United States could also have switched to production for domestic demand, a policy which would have required an aggressive attempt on the part of government to manage domestic demand. The depression years had shown again, however, the difficulty of developing a consensus in the United States for managing domestic demand. Any program of managed demand would involve, in one way or another, higher state spending and a turn toward planning and away from free enterprise—the exact opposite of the programs for fiscal austerity that have been the favorite medicine in the United States to cure any macroeconomic problem (as at the beginning of the depression and again in the 1970s).

If demand was to be maintained, higher postwar demand for U.S. exports was one of the few alternatives to greater state management. As Gabriel and Joyce Kolko explain in The Limits of Power, U.S. planners began during the war years to make estimates of the volume of exports necessary to keep U.S. industry at a tolerably high level of employment.

> From the 1932 low of $1.6 billion in exports, the United States attained $12.8 billion in 1943 and $14.3 billion in 1944, most of the new peak representing a favorable balance of trade. The figure of $14 billion in postwar exports—well over four times the 1939 level—therefore became the target of most wartime planners and their calculated precondition of continued American prosperity. [10]

U.S. exports of $14 billion would not, however, be balanced by $14 billion in imports. In plans as well as in postwar experience the United States would lend money to the governments of Europe and Japan to permit them to import several billion dollars more in U.S. goods than they could otherwise pay for at the time. The overall plan has an attractive logical unity: the United States used its loans for political leverage in the weakened countries of Europe and also for financing U.S. exports, thereby helping to maintain full employment in a United States that was as fearful of depression as it was of state planning to maintain demand.

Japan and Germany were potentially major industrial centers despite the severe setbacks they had suffered as losers in World War II. Because of their potential importance any scheme for organization of the world economy favorable to U.S. interests would reasonably have to include Japan and Germany as well. Their reconstruction under close U.S. sponsorship helped to insure the U.S. program of free trade and to discourage socialism and state planning, developments which would inhibit the activities of U.S. businesses throughout the world.

Two arguments have been presented here to explain the effort of the United States at the end of World War II to promote economic recovery in Western Europe and Japan. First, Western Europe (especially Germany) and Japan were considered to be strategic geopolitical barriers against Soviet expansion; U.S. aid and assistance helped to build strong allies. Second, Western Europe and Japan were potential markets for U.S. exports and their colonies were sources of needed raw materials; U.S. aid was used as a lever to help set up institutions of free world trade and multinational investment, insuring that the gigantic postwar U.S. industry could continue to grow on a world scale. Kennan's strategic explanation of U.S. aid is the establishment view and ties in closely with Cold War rhetoric. The Kolkos' explanation emphasizes economic motivation for political acts and is therefore leftist in tone. Both the left and the right agree that U.S. aid to Western Europe and to Japan, which was designed to speed economic recovery and growth in those areas, was at least in part a self-serving policy from the U.S. point of view. Economic growth both in Western Europe and in Japan was genuinely desired by the United States for its own reasons, either to hem in the Soviet Union (Kennan) or to help extend the worldwide influence of U.S. business (Kolko). Supine and weak economies in Europe and Japan were neither good allies nor good markets. The disagreement is wide between the left and right interpretation of U.S. policy, but the element of agreement is significant: by helping economic growth in Western Europe and Japan in the immediate postwar period the United States was helping itself.

A genuine desire to help the poor no doubt served as a motivation as well, but there were, and are now, many more and poorer people in India or Africa than in Western Europe and Japan. Pity and good will is a part, but only a part, of the explanation for U.S. aid to the recovery of Western Europe and Japan. The United States has never made an effort to aid economic growth elsewhere in the world that is comparable to the Marshall Plan and aid to Japan in terms of the percentage of GNP made available for aid.

THE STORY OF RELATIVE GROWTH RATES: WEST
GERMANY, JAPAN, AND THE UNITED STATES
FROM 1945 TO 1973

Although the entire noncommunist world experienced a period of rapid and relatively steady economic expansion from the late 1940s through the present, the growth rates have varied from one region to another. This variation in economic growth—however we wish to measure it—has changed the position of the United States in the world. Immediately after the war the United States was the giant industrial power among the noncommunist countries and in the world. By 1973 this situation had changed drastically. In the words of C. Fred Bergsten, former Assistant for International Economic Affairs on the Senior Staff of the National Security Council (1969–71), writing in early 1973,

> The international economic power . . . of the expanded European Community and Japan has been growing rapidly. Both are approaching the United States in their ability to achieve their international economic objectives, and both outstrip the United States on some key measures of international economic power.[11]

The changing relative position of the United States in international economics has understandably led to new U.S. attitudes. Businesses feel the competition of Japanese and West German exports in foreign markets and in the domestic market. U.S. strategic planners have come to realize that political resolve in West Germany and Japan can be backed up with economies that are large enough to present the United States with a serious challenge, whether in the economic sphere or perhaps even in the military sphere in years to come. Thus, the changing relative sizes of the economies of the United States, Japan, and West Germany have been the key element in shifting U.S. policies from unqualified support for economic expansion.

The change in U.S. policies occurred sometime in the late 1960s and early 1970s. By the late 1970s, conflict between Japan, West Germany, and the United States over international economic matters has become a consistent feature of international affairs. These conflicts overtly concern matters of international trade. A case could be made that the United States supports growth, but not certain trade policies that have been followed by Japan and West Germany; however, such arguments neglect two important facts. First, the troublesome trade policies of Japan and West Germany would not be so troublesome if those countries were weaker relative to the United States. It is an easy observation that further economic growth in Japan and West Germany will make their trade policies even more upsetting to the U.S. economy. Second, the growth plans of both West Germany and Japan envisioned consistently large trade surpluses from the late 1960s into the future. These surpluses, which would be used to expand foreign investments, were an integral part of the mature phase of economic growth planned by the economic councils of both countries. Such surpluses and foreign investments would mean lost sales and reduced business opportunities for U.S. firms. Consequently, although one could attempt to split hairs by arguing that West German and Japanese exports were the problem while economic growth was not, the argument is too refined. West German and Japanese growth, as planned and executed throughout the 1960s and 1970s, has presented a problem to U.S. business and to strategic planners in the U.S. government.

With the support of U.S. aid and with the help of the currency reform, the pace of postwar German recovery was exceedingly fast through the first half of 1951. By the second half of 1949, that part of Germany not under Soviet occupation (the British-, U.S.-, and French-occupied sections) had regained the GNP level of 1936, which may be taken as the baseline for prewar production. However, since the population of the Western-occupied sections of Germany had grown by about 25 percent from 1939 to 1954, largely through immigration of refugees, it took until 1951 for per capita GNP to recover to the 1936 level. [12]

From 1952 to 1973, GNP in West Germany (which was established as an independent government in September 1949) grew from 136.7 billion DM to 927.5 billion DM, or by a factor of 6.8. During the same period, the value of the deutsche mark relative to the dollar rose by about 57 percent (mostly from 1968 to 1973). If we use the exchange rate to translate current deutsche marks into current dollars, we find that the value of West German GNP in current dollars rose from 32.6 to 347.1 billion dollars; in 1973 German GNP in current dollars was 10.6 times what it was in 1952.

The case of Japan is even more striking. If we take production in 1934-36 as the baseline for prewar Japan, then by 1951 Japan had regained its prewar level of GNP. [13] From 1952 to 1973, Japan's GNP rose from 6.3 to 111.1 trillion yen, or by a factor of 17.6. In addition, the value of the yen rose against the dollar from 1952 to 1973 by 33 percent (yearly average of daily rates). This means that in terms of current dollars (using the exchange rate for the yen to translate current yen into current dollars) the GNP of Japan increased by a factor of 23.6 times from 1952 to 1973.

From 1952 to 1973, while the GNPs of Japan and West Germany were increasing by over ten and twenty times, respectively, in terms of current dollar equivalents, the GNP of the United States increased by a mere 3.8 times (Table 2.1). Although current dollar equivalents cannot be used to measure real growth, the changing ratios of GNPs— even in current dollar equivalents—can be used to measure changes in relative real size. For example, the relative size of the GNP of Japan compared with that of the United States has changed by a factor

TABLE 2.1

U.S., West German, and Japanese GNP, 1952-73

	United States	West Germany			Japan		
	Current GNP (billion U.S.$)	Current GNP (billion DM)	Exchange Rate (DM/U.S.$)	Current GNP (billion U.S.$)	Current GNP (billion Y)	Exchange Rate (Y/U.S.$)	Current GNP (billion U.S.$)
1952	347.2	136.7	4.20	32.6	6,263	361	17.3
1953	366.1	147.1	4.20	35.1	7,055	361	19.6
1954	366.3	157.8	4.20	37.6	7,831	361	21.7
1955	399.3	180.4	4.21	42.9	8,624	361	23.9
1956	420.7	198.8	4.20	47.3	9,726	360	27.0
1957	442.8	216.3	4.20	51.5	11,083	360	30.8
1958	448.9	231.5	4.19	55.3	11,521	360	32.0
1959	486.5	250.6	4.18	60.0	12,926	360	35.9
1960	506.0	302.3	4.17	72.5	15,487	360	43.0
1961	523.3	332.6	4.02	82.8	19,124	361	53.0
1962	563.8	360.1	4.00	90.1	21,202	361	58.8
1963	594.7	384.0	3.97	96.3	24,475	361	67.7
1964	635.7	420.9	3.98	105.9	28,916	362	79.9
1965	688.1	460.4	3.99	115.3	31,953	361	88.4
1966	753.0	490.7	4.00	122.7	36,822	362	101.6
1967	796.3	495.5	3.99	124.3	43,570	362	120.3
1968	868.5	540.0	3.99	135.3	51,600	361	143.1
1969	935.1	605.2	3.92	154.2	59,669	358	166.5
1970	982.4	685.6	3.65	188.0	70,709	358	197.4
1971	1,063.4	761.9	3.48	218.8	79,258	349	227.2
1972	1,171.1	833.9	3.18	261.5	90,621	308	294.2
1973	1,306.6	927.5	2.67	347.1	111,034	272	407.9

Source: International Monetary Fund (IMF), International Financial Statistics 30, 5 (Washington, D.C.: IMF, May 1977), pp. 174-77, 234-37, 400-3.

of 6.2. From being one twentieth the size of the U.S. economy in 1952, by 1973 the Japanese economy was approaching a third the size of the U.S. economy. Similarly, the economy of West Germany in 1952 was about one eleventh the size of the U.S. economy but by 1973 had grown to be just over a quarter. By 1973 West Germany had grown in relative size by a factor of 2.8. To help put the relative sizes in 1952 into perspective, we can note that in 1973 Brazil's economy was 6 percent as large as the U.S. economy, while in 1952 Japan's economy was only 5 percent as large as the U.S. economy, and West Germany's was only 9 percent as large.

Figures of GNP, however, are blunt tools with which to examine the growing economic conflict between Japan, West Germany, and the United States. Real GNP shows the foundation for confrontation; the confrontation itself is more closely examined in real flows of goods between countries.

In 1952, the U.S. share of world exports among members of the International Monetary Fund—which excludes most, but not all, communist countries, but includes nearly all others—was 20.8 percent by value (Table 2.2). The share of world exports for West Germany and Japan for the same year was 5.5 and 1.7 percent, respectively. By 1973, the share of world exports for the United States had fallen to 13.6 percent, and in the same year Japan had 7.1 percent of world exports, and West Germany had 12.9 percent of world exports.

Throughout the 1950s and 1960s, exports as a percent of GNP stayed relatively constant at about 4 percent. For Japan and West Germany, exports as a share of GNP showed a very slight upward trend. For Japan the share increased from about 7 percent to 10 percent from 1952 to 1971. For Germany the share increased from about 12 percent in 1952 to about 18 percent in 1971. In other words, most of the increased share of world export markets for Japan and West Germany must be explained simply by total growth and cannot be attributed to export-oriented growth or to aggressive penetration of foreign markets, although that may appear to be the case to someone unaware of the tremendous economic advance underway in those two countries.

A closer examination of exports and imports by commodity classification gives an even clearer picture of the growing confrontation (Table 2.3). For Japan and West Germany in 1973, about 81 percent of their exports were manufactures, while only 26 percent of Japanese imports and 51 percent of West German imports were manufactured goods. For the United States, only 63 percent of exports in 1973 and as much as 60 percent of imports consisted of manufactured goods. According to the classical pattern for industrial states, Japan and West Germany import food and raw materials and

TABLE 2.2

U.S., West German, and Japanese Exports, 1952–73

	United States		West Germany		Japan	
	Percent of GNP	Percent of Total World Exports	Percent of GNP	Percent of Total World Exports	Percent of GNP	Percent of Total World Exports
1952	4.4	20.8	12.4	5.5	7.3	1.7
1953	4.3	21.3	12.6	5.9	6.5	1.7
1954	4.1	19.7	14.0	6.8	7.5	2.1
1955	3.9	18.7	14.3	7.3	8.4	2.4
1956	4.5	20.6	15.5	7.9	9.3	2.7
1957	4.8	20.9	16.6	8.6	9.3	2.9
1958	4.0	18.8	15.9	9.3	9.0	3.0
1959	3.6	17.5	16.4	9.7	9.6	3.4
1960	4.1	18.2	15.7	10.1	9.4	3.7
1961	4.0	17.8	15.3	10.6	8.0	3.6
1962	3.9	17.5	14.7	10.7	8.4	4.0
1963	3.9	17.2	15.1	10.7	8.1	4.0
1964	4.2	17.5	15.3	10.6	8.4	4.4
1965	4.0	16.6	15.5	10.8	9.6	5.1
1966	4.0	16.8	16.4	11.1	9.6	5.4
1967	4.0	16.6	17.5	11.4	8.7	5.5
1968	4.0	16.2	18.4	11.6	9.1	6.1
1969	4.1	15.6	18.7	11.8	9.6	6.5
1970	4.4	15.4	18.2	12.2	9.8	6.8
1971	4.1	14.1	17.9	12.5	10.6	7.7
1972	4.2	13.2	17.8	12.4	9.7	7.6
1973	5.5	13.6	19.5	12.9	9.1	7.1

Source: International Monetary Fund, International Financial Statistics 30, 5 (Washington, D.C.: IMF, May 1977), pp. 56–57, 174–77, 234–37, 400–3.

TABLE 2.3

Composition of Exports and Imports for the United States, Japan, and West Germany by Major Categories
(percent)

	Exports				Imports		
	Food	Other Agricultural Products	Minerals	Manufactures and Others	Food and Raw Materials	Fuels and Lubricants	Total Manufactures
United States							
1960	15.7	9.0	12.9	59.4	52.4	10.5	37.1
1965	21.1	5.5	10.4	63.0	45.2	10.4	44.4
1970	16.0	4.9	12.1	67.0	33.5	7.7	58.8
1973	23.5	5.6	7.8	63.1	28.8	11.7	59.5
Japan							
1960	7.6	3.0	10.6	79.0	65.7	16.5	17.8
1965	4.4	2.6	17.1	75.9	62.2	19.9	17.9
1970	3.3	1.7	16.0	79.0	55.4	20.7	23.9
1973	2.2	1.8	15.2	80.8	52.6	21.8	25.6
West Germany							
1960	2.3	2.1	19.7	75.9	59.6	7.7	32.7
1965	2.8	1.8	15.2	80.2	48.6	7.8	43.6
1970	3.4	1.5	13.4	81.7	42.1	8.8	49.2
1973	4.5	1.7	12.6	81.2	37.7	11.4	50.9

Source: World Bank, World Tables 1976 (Baltimore: Johns Hopkins Press, 1976), pp. 454–55, 462–63.

export manufactured articles, but the United States has moved to a position where it imports nearly as much in manufactured articles as it exports.

Toward the end of the 1960s, the industrial potentials of Japan and Western Europe began to impress themselves on the world. The challenge to U.S. industrial exports developed rapidly. In Japan, growth actually accelerated as a higher percentage of GNP was plowed back in investment. The comfortable notion that Japanese and Western European growth rates were pulled along by technology transfer from the United States had to be scrutinized more carefully. According to such a notion, the wealthy United States grows more slowly because it has to find the way, whereas Japan and West Germany following behind are able to imitate rather than innovate and, hence, can grow faster. But as Japan and several European countries approached U.S. levels of output, the anticipated slowdown was not to be seen.

Looking at West Germany and Japan in the late 1960s and early 1970s, one saw a range of heavy industries in which the United States had already lost its lead: in terms of per capita production of cement, crude steel, and plastics, both Japan and West Germany had surpassed the United States by 1970.[14] The sinews of industry in Japan and West Germany were strong; it was no longer a catch-up game.

If trends in economic growth were to continue, it was possible to foresee that by the time an American who was 30 years old in 1973 finished his or her working life and retired the United States would have an overall GNP less than that of either Japan or West Germany; but since the population of the United States would be so much larger than the populations of either of the other two countries, the real GNP per capita of the United States would be less than half that of Japan or West Germany. The U.S. share of world exports of manufactures would by similar extrapolation fall to half or less than that of either Japan or West Germany.

The West German and Japanese challenges inherent in such projections of present growth rates began to impress themselves on U.S. strategic planners at the end of the 1960s. What policy responses the United States will resort to in an attempt to alter the march of compound growth rates is a major question that should underlie examinations of U.S. foreign policy in the 1970s and 1980s. As one author has noted in reference to Japanese growth, the possibilities are ominous.

America's military defeat in Vietnam will be followed over the next 15 years by a series of economic defeats in the race with Japan: she will be dethroned as richest in the world in annual flow per capita, as the No. 1 exporter, as the world's financial centre, with Japan's so-called foreign aid programme being double or triple America's sums, and with Japan gaining bigger and bigger market shares in Asia, Africa, South America, Europe—with US market shares steadily dwindling.

Can the Americans be expected to applaud these defeats? How hysterical will they become?
We do not know. [15]

COOPERATION GIVES WAY TO CONFRONTATION

In the late 1960s, strengthened by their tremendous efforts at industrial growth, both Japan and West Germany attempted to move into a large and consistent surplus position in international trade. The surpluses of Japan and West Germany were designed to pay for foreign investments, foreign aid, and in general for the exercise of economic power in international affairs. As losers in World War II, both nations lost assets beyond their borders. As growing industrial giants, both nations wanted and continue to want footholds on resources and markets in foreign countries—footholds that they can attain peaceably through international investment, that is, through purchase. But in order to purchase foreign assets they must export to earn foreign exchange. Hence, for both countries, in the 1970s the plan to run consistent surpluses was an integral and essential part of their strategy of economic growth.

Throughout the 1950s and 1960s the United States had run consistent surpluses on international trade, exporting more goods than were imported. The United States had received as well substantial income on foreign investments. These receipts permitted the United States to finance various international activities such as foreign investment, foreign aid, foreign military bases, and military ventures. For Japan and West Germany to attempt to run consistently large surpluses was for them to try to do nothing more than the United States had done for years. It is unfortunate for the stability of world economic relations that all nations cannot run large trade surpluses at the same time; the attempt by all three to attain large surpluses led to competition for markets and eventually to confrontation.

Shifts in trade balances from 1956 to 1973 for the United States, Japan, and West Germany provide a clear picture of the developing confrontation (Table 2.4). Until 1966, the trade surpluses of West Germany were seldom more than one-third of the U.S. trade surplus. Meanwhile, Japan was frequently in deficit through 1961 and did not begin to run consistent surpluses until 1964. Then, in a few short years the surpluses of both Japan and West Germany vaulted past those of the United States. The trade surplus of West Germany passed that of the United States in 1967, and West German surpluses have exceeded U.S. surpluses ever since. In 1968, the trade surpluses of Japan also drove past those of the United States and have stayed ahead in every year but 1975. In 1971 the United States ran a trade deficit in the face of a $12-billion aggregate trade surplus for Japan and West Germany.

TABLE 2.4

Trade Balances of the United States, Japan,
and West Germany, 1956-73
(f.o.b.)

	United States	Japan	West Germany*
1956	4,574	-125	697
1957	6,099	-395	980
1958	3,313	-376	1,162
1959	988	365	1,215
1960	4,757	271	1,264
1961	5,429	-558	1,623
1962	4,417	401	767
1963	5,057	-166	1,413
1964	6,801	374	1,351
1965	4,951	1,901	248
1966	3,817	2,275	2,956
1967	3,800	1,160	5,252
1968	635	2,529	5,676
1969	607	3,699	5,158
1970	2,603	3,963	5,691
1971	-2,252	7,787	6,363
1972	-6,415	8,971	8,360
1973	873	3,694	15,337

*Values c.i.f. for 1956-65.
Sources: International Monetary Fund, International Financial Statistics 30, 5 (Washington, D.C.: IMF, May 1977), pp. 176-77, 236-67, 402-3, and 30, 11 (November 1977), pp. 150-51; International Monetary Fund, Balance of Payments Yearbook, vol. 23 (Washington, D.C.: IMF, 1972), section for West Germany, p. 7.

The struggle for trade surpluses eventually led to the end of the Bretton Woods system in 1971. According to the Bretton Woods system, designed toward the end of World War II under U.S. leadership, governments were obliged to cooperate in setting mutually acceptable exchange rates for their currencies and to maintain fixed relative values by standing ready to buy (with gold, U.S. dollars, or other foreign currency) or to sell their own currency at the fixed exchange rate. Rates were not, however, immutable; if for some reason the value of a currency were too low (or too high), its value could be increased by simply giving it a higher price in terms of other currencies, a maneuver known as revaluation (or decreased by giving it a lower price, known as devaluation). For our purposes, the Bretton Woods system may be understood as a system of "gentlemen's agreements" on currency values. To say that the Bretton Woods system broke down means nothing more nor less than that the major nations were unable to agree on the relative values of their currencies.

In the late 1960s, with U.S. industries being squeezed by West German and Japanese goods, U.S. government officials felt that the situation could be improved for the United States if West Germany and Japan would revalue—increase the cost of—their currency and thereby increase the cost of their exports in foreign markets. High prices for West German and Japanese exports would give U.S. businesses the advantage they needed to rebuild the U.S. trade surplus. But since West Germany and Japan were more than happy with their trade surpluses, they were unwilling to revalue. (West Germany did revalue 10 percent in 1969, but that was not sufficient either to satisfy the United States or to help the U.S. trade balance.)

Demand for Japanese and West German goods in the late 1960s and early 1970s led to excess demand for the deutsche mark and the yen. The central banks of Japan and West Germany willingly supplied yen and deutsche marks, receiving dollars in exchange. As the trade surpluses continued for Japan and West Germany, the dollar balances in the central banks of Japan and West Germany accumulated. Such dollar balances in foreign central banks are a symptom of disagreement over trade patterns; we see them again in the late 1970s.

In 1974 Helmut Schmidt, Minister of Finance and later Chancellor of West Germany, related the breakdown of the Bretton Woods system to the payments deficits of the United States (which we must remember were due to the faltering trade balances of the United States).

Ultimately, the system broke down because it failed to provide the framework for an orderly exchange of goods

and services. Bretton Woods benefitted some countries more than others—particularly the strong more
than the weak—and above all it burdened the international monetary system with the payments deficits of
the superpower. [16]

For Helmut Schmidt to blame the breakdown of Bretton Woods
on the United States for running trade deficits is grossly misleading.
West Germany and Japan accumulated dollars against the wishes of
the United States, which would rather have seen both the yen and the
deutsche mark revalued. But if West Germany and Japan had not
accumulated dollar balances they could not have run the large trade
surpluses they so badly desired. Schmidt's analysis must be turned
on its head to make any sense: the Bretton Woods system—the regime of "gentlemen's agreements" on the value of important currencies—broke down because West Germany and Japan insisted on forcing the United States into trade deficits once they had become powerful enough to insist on large surpluses for themselves. The deficits
that Helmut Schmidt charges obliquely to U.S. machinations were
not wanted and did not benefit the United States. [17]

That the United States was concerned to get rid of the deficits
and that such an attempt was blocked by West Germany and Japan is
apparent from the denouement of the Bretton Woods system, en-
gineered in 1971 by President Nixon. The trend toward U.S. trade
deficits and toward large trade surpluses in Japan and West Germany
had prompted increasingly agitated complaints among U.S. business
and government economists in 1970 and 1971. It was a case of un-
fair competition, the industrialists claimed. Nixon chose to respond
to all the nation's economic woes with a program of domestic and international policies designed to gain political support in the United
States through their bold and forceful presentation. He unveiled his
entire program on August 15, 1971, in a speech to the nation. He
announced the U.S. intention to devalue, but left it up to other countries to change the values of their currencies relative to the dollar;
the intention was to have the dollar devalued primarily against the
deutsche mark and the yen, without having to change the relative
value of the dollar with all other currencies. In order to force Japan
and West Germany to revalue according to U.S. wishes, Nixon put
an extra import duty on all manufactured imports; this duty was to
be removed when the United States was satisfied with the new exchange rates. The duty was clearly against international treaties
and understandings that the United States had signed. The Nixon
economic program was unsettling to the world economy, and it was
announced to the world in a rude and challenging manner; the whole
package was designed for shock value.

In Japan, the stock market fell in the next eight days about 20 percent from its value before the Nixon speech. Investors in Japan lost a total of $16 billion; the shock of the August 15 speech on U.S. economic policy followed by only a month the first Nixon shock—the announcement of his impending visit to China. In both cases, the policy changes were kept a secret even from leading Japanese officials until just minutes before the public announcement.

Of the Japanese mood in 1971 after the new U.S. international economic policies were announced, one foreign resident wrote,

> For several months, there is a heavy blanket of mourning over the islands of Japan: what people mourned was the belief that the United States harboured friendly feelings towards Japan. . . . This is a cruel autumn for Japan: an autumn of loneliness, in which Japan experiences a feeling of being expelled from the community of nations, this time for having been too successful in peacetime competition. [18]

Japan was not the only nation shocked by the calculated effort of the United States to destabilize the system and to improve U.S. trade prospects. C. Fred Bergsten, who was an economic advisor to the National Security Council until May 1971, noted general distress with U.S. behavior:

> Confidence in the entire fabric of international economic cooperation nearly collapsed in late 1971, when it took four months to resolve the crisis triggered by the United States actions of August 15. Throughout the world, investment plans and economic projects plummeted. The British prime minister refused to meet the American president at the [economic] summit [in late 1971] until the United States took steps toward ending the economic suspense. [19]

Devaluation of the dollar and revaluation of the deutsche mark and yen from August 1971 to the middle of 1973 added over a third to the value of the mark and yen relative to the dollar. With these changes, the U.S. trade balance improved between 1971 and 1973 from a $2.3-billion deficit to a $0.9-billion surplus. But the improvement in West Germany's trade balance for the same period (from a $6.4-billion surplus in 1971 to a $15.3-billion surplus in 1973) was greater. Although Japan suffered a deterioration in its trade balance, the Japanese economy continued to grow quickly: the rate of growth of real GNP for 1972 was 8.9 percent and for 1973 was 9.8 percent. Confrontation in international monetary matters had proven ineffective; the United States was losing its economic lead and found itself with a consistently declining share of world economic power.

Then in late 1973 the world was rocked with the oil embargo and several stiff oil-price increases. Whatever the U.S. government's policy on the oil-price increases, the simple fact is that the United States was hurt less than were Japan or West Germany. In the price increases of 1973 and the events surrounding them, it is not too difficult to see strains among the noncommunist industrial powers. Whether the increases are in any way related to the late 1960s and early 1970s shift in U.S. economic policies toward confrontation with Japan and West Germany is a question that deserves careful consideration.

Whatever the conclusion on oil prices (which are discussed in Chapter 3), in other matters the United States has revealed a clear change in attitude toward economic growth in Japan and West Germany. In the immediate postwar period, the United States as the preeminent industrial power nurtured Japan and West Germany along a path of high economic growth. Strategic advantages accrued to the United States through the growing strength of its allies, and economic advantages accrued to U.S. business through exports and the profitability of foreign investment (especially in Europe). But by the late 1960s the United States saw economic competition and became wary of the growing economic power and independence of Western European countries and Japan. Instead of offering aid, the United States complained of competition and attempted, at least through monetary confrontation, to improve its own position at the expense of Japan and West Germany.

NOTES

1. Häkan Hedberg, Japan's Revenge (London: Pitman, 1972), p. 24.

2. This section relies very heavily on the memoirs of George F. Kennan, Memoirs 1925-1950 (Boston: Little, Brown, 1967). Kennan was head of the Policy Planning Staff of the State Department from 1947 to 1949.

3. Ibid., p. 368.

4. Ibid., p. 333.

5. Henry Wallich, Mainsprings of the German Revival (New Haven: Yale University Press, 1955), p. 36.

6. Ibid., p. 15.

7. Ibid., p. 67.

8. Kennan, p. 395.

9. This section relies heavily on the interpretation of American foreign policy in Gabriel Kolko and Joyce Kolko, The Limits of Power: The World and United States Foreign Policy 1945-1954 (New York: Harper & Row, 1972).

10. Ibid., p. 21.

11. C. Fred Bergsten and John A. Mathieson, "The Future of the International Economic Order," in The Future of the International Economic Order, ed. C. Fred Bergsten (Lexington, Mass.: Lexington, 1973), p. 6.

12. Wallich, p. 36.

13. George C. Allen, A Short Economic History of Modern Japan 1867-1937 (London: Allen & Unwin, 1972), p. 244.

14. Hedberg, Table I (App.).

15. Ibid., p. 174.

16. Helmut Schmidt, "The Struggle for the World Product," in The World Economic Crisis, ed. William Bundy (New York: Norton, 1975), p. 106.

17. "The United States was not fundamentally dissatisfied until it lost its surplus on current account." Robert O. Keohane and Joseph S. Nye, "World Politics and the International Economic System," in Bergsten, p. 134.

18. Hedberg, pp. 52-53.

19. Bergsten and Mathieson, p. 7.

3

AN EXPLANATION OF THE OIL CRISIS

American oil operations are, for all practical purposes,
instruments of our foreign policy toward these countries
[the Middle East oil-exporting countries].

> Department of State report, backed by
> Defense and Interior, to the National
> Security Council in January 1953.[1]

In the late 1940s and early 1950s, the government of Iran
quarreled with the British oil company, British Petroleum,[2] which
had rights to 100 percent of Iran's oil. Iranian disfavor with BP
was supported by the American ambassador, "who encouraged
Iranians . . . to believe that the Americans would support them
against the British."[3] In 1951, under the leadership of Dr. Mossadeq,
the newly elected prime minister, the Iranian government national-
ized the company's assets in Iran and prepared to sell the oil on its
own.

In forming a response to the Iranian nationalization, the
British government sought the prior consent of the U.S. government.
The United States strongly discouraged force against Iran, and although Britain had made some military preparations nothing was
done. The flow of oil from Iran, however, was thoroughly stopped.
The usual interpretation is that this was accomplished through a
boycott by the major oil companies, but this cannot be correct. To
stop the export of oil out of Iran involved not a boycott but a blockade:
British warplanes prevented oil tankers from transporting Iranian
oil. This exercise of military power by Britain was sufficient to
discourage most nations (and/or their companies) from buying
Iranian oil. The consent of the vastly more powerful United States
to respect the blockade could not have been forced; for its own
reasons the United States cooperated.

The blockade operated for two years, effectively preventing
oil exports. Meanwhile, no success was achieved in attempts to

strike a bargain with Mossadeq. In 1953, the United States and
Great Britain cooperated in supporting a coup in Iran, throwing out
Mossadeq and reestablishing the Shah. The CIA chief in Iran,
Kermit Roosevelt, a grandson of Theodore Roosevelt, is universally
given credit for directing the coup. Since 1953 he has been known
as "Mr. Iran" in the CIA.

The end of the blockade illustrates the motives and payoffs
for U.S. actions throughout. In negotiations to establish new arrangements for foreign oil companies to handle Iranian oil, the five
largest U.S. international oil companies were pushed into the picture by the U.S. State Department. The agreement under which oil
flow was resumed brought in U.S. companies for 40 percent of what
had formerly been an all-British concession.

U.S. military power was instrumental at several points in the
transformation of British Petroleum's sole ownership of the Iranian
concession into a joint venture that included U.S. companies. First,
the United States encouraged Iranians to move against the British.
Second, the United States discouraged Britain from forcible interference in Iran. Third, the United States cooperated (whether de
factor or by prior agreement) with the oil blockade of Iran that was
enforced by the British. Fourth, the United States participated in
the coup that overthrew Mossadeq. That the United States only took
40 percent for its efforts shows diplomatic restraint designed to
protect good relations with Great Britain.

In 1970 a similar situation appeared to be developing in Libya,
this time with several U.S. companies feeling particularly threatened. The different response on the part of the United States in
1970 as compared with that of Britain in 1951 is instructive. Colonel
Quaddafi, who had come to power in a coup in 1969, began in early
1970 to demand higher taxes from the oil companies. The U.S.
government considered tempting Libya to nationalize and forcing
them to yield through preventing oil exports. According to James
Akins, the top oil expert in the State Department, the main reason
that such a course of action was not followed was that Western
European nations would not have cooperated.

> We in the State Department had no doubt whatever at
> that time . . . that the Europeans would have made
> their own deals with the Libyans; and that they would
> have paid the higher taxes Libya demanded and that the
> Anglo-Saxon oil companies' sojourn in Libya would
> have ended. [4]

While the British blockade supported by the United States
would work against Iran in 1951, a blockade against Libya in 1970

was not attempted. The reason that such a course of action—possible in 1951—was considered dangerous in 1970 was not that anything had changed in the oil-exporting countries (growing nationalism or militancy, for example), but rather that important countries of Western Europe (France, Italy, and West Germany) were much more powerful and independent in 1970 than in 1951, and they may have been willing to test the blockade to protect their oil supplies. With any blockade there would have been the possibility that the United States would be faced with a choice of whether or not to use force against, for example, a French tanker with military escort.

The situations in Iran and in Libya together illustrate that the exercise of power in defense of oil interests does not involve in its primary manifestation an invasion or even the potential for invasion. The essential exercise of power is against other potential contractors for oil and against other nations attempting to buy oil. In 1970 negotiations with Libya, the major concern of the U.S. government—overriding the matters of taxes and nationalizations—was to maintain the dominant presence of U.S. oil companies against the perceived intentions of Western European nations to interfere should they be given the chance.

The willingness of other oil-importing nations to interfere in Libya enabled Libya to get more money and a share of U.S. oil companies in Libya. The United States, however, had reasons to agree as well as to object: in the face of the increasingly wealthy, independent, and powerful countries of Western Europe and Japan, U.S. interests favored a regime of much higher oil prices together with participation by the producer countries to supplement, validate, and maintain the U.S.-dominated company cartel in the face of the increasing resentment of Western Europe and Japan. But to make sense of the U.S. role in the 1973 price increases, we must begin the story much before 1970.

TWO PERIODS OF U.S. DOMINANCE IN OIL

The first oil well has been credited by American tradition to Colonel Drake, drilling in Ohio in 1859. The story is far from true, for oil has been taken from wells in Burma, Rumania, and other countries for centuries, but it is at least figuratively true for the modern oil industry. Oil production in the United States dominates the story of the early modern oil industry; until the 1880s, the U.S. share of total world oil production remained above 85 percent (Table 3.1).

The history of U.S. oil very quickly became the history of John D. Rockefeller. The Standard Oil trust was put together by

TABLE 3.1

Major Oil-Producing Areas, 1860–1975

	United States		Venezuela and Mexico*		Middle East and North Africa		Russia/Soviet Union		World Total
	1,000 bbl./day	Percent of World Production	1,000 bbl./day	Percent of World Production	1,000 bbl./day	Percent of World Production	1,000 bbl./day	Percent of World Production	
1860	1.4	98.4	—	—	—	—	—	—	1.4
1870	14	90.7	—	—	—	—	.6	3.5	16
1880	72	87.6	—	—	—	—	8.2	10.0	82
1890	126	59.8	—	—	—	—	79	37.4	210
1900	174	42.7	—	—	—	—	208	50.9	408
1910	574	63.9	10	1.1	—	—	193	21.4	898
1920	1,214	64.3	430	22.8	34	1.8	70	3.7	1,899
1930	2,460	63.6	483	12.5	128	3.3	344	8.9	3,868
1940	3,707	62.9	510	8.6	260	4.4	600	10.2	5,890
1950	5,408	51.9	1,499	14.4	512	16.2	729	7.0	10,420
1960	7,055	36.1	2,855	14.6	4,778	24.4	2,822	14.4	19,542
1970	9,637	21.0	3,708	8.1	18,627	40.7	7,070	15.4	45,804
1975	8,362	15.7	2,346	4.4	22,321	41.8	9,800	18.3	53,418

* Mexico only until 1930.

Sources: 1860–1960: Harvey O'Connor, World Crisis in Oil (New York: Monthly Review Press, 1962), pp. 19, 46, 61, 90; 1970–75: U.S. Department of the Interior, Bureau of Mines, International Petroleum Annual 1975 (Washington, D.C.: Department of the Interior, 1977), pp. 24–25; Soviet Union, 1970–75: Central Intelligence Agency, National Foreign Assessment Center, International Energy Statistical Review (Washington, D.C.: Central Intelligence Agency, 1978), p. 24. (To get the figures for Soviet oil production in 1970 and 1975, I have added Soviet exports and consumption of oil.)

Rockefeller in the early 1880s. Rockefeller imposed order on oil refining and marketing, largely eliminating the cycle of boom and bust that had characterized oil in its early years of wildcatting and small-scale operations. Rockefeller's Standard Oil trust was officially broken up according to an antitrust ruling handed down in 1911. Since World War II, three of the many remnants of the former Standard Oil trust have been among the "seven sisters" group of major world oil companies; these three are Exxon (formerly Standard Oil of New Jersey), Mobil (formerly Standard Oil of New York), and Socal (formerly Standard Oil of California).

The early oil industry was a U.S. preserve because of the United States' position as the largest producer in the world. Russian oil grew quickly toward the end of the nineteenth century, and for a time at the turn of the century Russia had displaced the United States as the world's largest producer of oil. Although Russian oil escaped from the clutches of Rockefeller's Standard Oil trust, it did not escape other competing organizations of control and supervision. Oil has always been a big-money business, both because it made millionaires and because it attracted them. The oil of Russia was developed by Nobels and Rothschilds and was sold to several emerging European oil corporations. Shell Oil bought Russian oil and shipped it southeast through the Suez Canal to the markets of Asia. The necessary permission to ship oil through the Suez Canal was gained by Shell at least in part because it was a British company. With its European sources and its Far East markets, Shell grew into a world power in oil in the late nineteenth and early twentieth centuries.

In 1890 Royal Dutch Petroleum received a royal charter and began to fight for oil markets with its oil from the Dutch East Indies. In 1906, the Royal Dutch Petroleum Company and Shell Oil Company merged to form Royal Dutch/Shell with 40 percent British ownership against 60 percent Dutch ownership. Headquarters for the company have been located in England since its formation.

Another early oil company, the Anglo-Persian Oil Company, grew into a major company early in the twentieth century with the help and participation of the British government. British Petroleum, as Anglo-Persian became known, received in 1914 official British government support in the form of 51 percent ownership and an arrangement to supply oil for the British navy. The plum for BP from 1908 until 1951 was its 100 percent control of the reserves for Iran.

The preeminent position of U.S. companies (that is, Rockefeller's Standard Oil trust) in world oil trade had been reached in the nineteenth century. Before the turn of the century, the European colonial powers with their greater access to sources of oil throughout the world were able to enter into competition in Asian, South Asian, and European markets. Governments of home countries in all cases played a part in aiding the competitive position of their companies. Although Rockefeller was able to maintain large market shares, especially in kerosene for lamps and oil for lubricants, his foreign operations suffered from the relative military and diplomatic weakness of the United States in Asia and the Middle East. U.S. companies were especially hampered in their efforts to acquire oil-producing concessions outside of the United States. Until 1928 the Dutch and the British kept them out of the Dutch East Indies and the Middle East, respectively. Before 1900, American companies had no foreign oil, and by 1914 foreign oil produced by U.S. oil companies accounted for only 15 percent of total world production outside of the United States.[5]

World War I illustrated the importance of oil in world power: in Lord Curzon's famous phrase, "The Allies floated to victory on a wave of oil." Production in the United States expanded to supply the Allies with oil for the war effort. Partly as a consequence of expanded production, the United States began to fear a shortage of future oil supplies, and that fear of shortage was translated into U.S. interest in foreign sources of oil. Although domestic U.S. production in 1920 was nearly two-thirds of total world production (see Table 3.1), and U.S. exports of oil supplied over a third of total non-U.S. consumption,[6] the U.S. government was nevertheless dissatisfied with the small share of foreign oil production that was under the control of U.S. oil companies. Consequently, after the war the U.S. government began to push hard for U.S. companies to be permitted entry into concessions in the Middle East and elsewhere.

At the end of World War I, the Turkish Empire was broken up and Iraq was given to the British as a mandated territory (that is, temporary colony). Since Germany had acquired some rights to Iraqi (or Turkish) oil before World War I, its share had to be reassigned as one of the spoils of war, and this necessitated the renegotiation of the concession. In 1928, when the Iraq Petroleum Company was formed, Exxon and Mobil were together given 23.75 percent of the oil found in the concession; the agreement represented the first time any U.S. company had gained access to Middle East oil. The French were also given an identical interest of 23.75 percent to be held by Compagnie Française de Pétrole (CFP). The British kept two shares of 23.75 percent each, one for BP and one for Royal Dutch/Shell. The remaining 5 percent belonged to Calouste Gulbenkian, an individual entrepreneur with important connections in the Middle East.

At least one of the levers which were used to help Standard Oil of New Jersey (or Exxon) and Standard Oil of New York (or Mobil) gain access to the Iraq concession is entirely clear: the

U.S. government took an active role in arguing that the United States deserved a share of the Turkish Empire—or at least of its oil resources—for having participated in World War I on the winning side. As part of its diplomatic effort, the U.S. government threatened to support Turkey's claim to the mandated territory of Iraq if Britain did not share the oil with U.S. companies.

Also in 1928 diplomatic efforts on behalf of U.S. oil companies in their attempt to gain access to oil in the Dutch East Indies finally bore fruit. One lever which had been used was the denial of domestic oil concessions to Shell (partly Dutch-owned) until U.S. companies were admitted into the Dutch East Indies.

Despite these successes, U.S. companies' share of total world output outside the United States had dropped from over half to less than 30 percent from 1920 to 1929. In 1929 U.S. companies accounted for only 3 percent of oil production in the eastern hemisphere. Without substantial eastern hemisphere production, the U.S. position in world oil was based in 1929 on exports of U.S. oil (30 percent of non-U.S. demand) and on production in Venezuela, where U.S. companies owned over half of the production in what was then the largest oil-producing nation in the world after the United States.[7]

During the 1920s a major price war broke out in South Asia. Price wars and disorderly competition quickly spread to oil markets around the world. Although Standard Oil of New Jersey had for years consistently resisted efforts by Royal Dutch/Shell to set up long-term cartel arrangements, by the late 1920s the position of Standard of New Jersey, in the face of rising production outside the control of U.S. companies, had deteriorated to the point where further conflict looked uninviting. Consequently, the leaders of Royal Dutch/Shell, British Petroleum, and Standard Oil of New Jersey met together and successfully concluded a general agreement about market shares in the world. The agreement of 1928 among the "big three" of world oil is known as the "Achnacarry Agreement," after the Scottish castle where the oil barons met, or the "As Is" agreement, for its general design was to freeze market shares as they were. It represented a formalization of cartel behavior, the end of price wars between the majors, and a rough parity for the big three in oil.

The growing power of the United States, together with the declining power of Great Britain, was within two decades to lead to a new share of power between five U.S. companies, Royal Dutch/Shell, and British Petroleum. The share of the world oil market held by U.S. companies relative to the other two members of the former big three would also increase. This push by the American oil companies was supported by the State Department, made possible by the vast financial resources of the U.S. companies from their domestic business, and successful in part through luck in locating major new oil fields in Kuwait and Saudi Arabia. But the ultimate deciding influence of U.S. military power, especially in the post-World War II period, cannot be overemphasized.

Throughout the 1930s, aggressive action on the part of Gulf Oil and of Standard Oil of California (Socal), supported when necessary by the State Department, brought them into possession of concessions in Bahrain, Saudi Arabia, and Kuwait. Oil was found in Bahrain in 1932 and in Saudi Arabia and Kuwait in 1938. Although there were small commercial exports during the 1930s, World War II intervened before Middle East production outside of Iran got off the ground. As late as 1945, Saudi Arabia produced less than 1 percent of world oil, Iraq only a little over 1 percent, and Iran about 5 percent; other Middle East production was negligible. Nevertheless, despite the small prewar contribution to world oil production from the Middle East, U.S. government planners during World War II fully realized the coming importance of the Middle East in world oil.

One important country for U.S. plans in the Middle East was Saudi Arabia. For a time during the war the United States, under the urging of Secretary of the Interior Ickes, considered a plan for a 100 percent U.S.-government-owned company to develop Saudi oil. Although initial steps were taken to set up the company, the plan was never carried through. Instead, the U.S. State Department worked after the war to get two more major U.S. oil companies, Exxon and Mobil, into the Saudi Arabian concession along with Socal and Texaco. (Texaco had been admitted in 1936 to help Socal market the expected flow of oil.) Most of the oil of Saudi Arabia, which by 1973 was producing over 25 percent of all OPEC oil, has been produced and marketed by four U.S. companies.

In Iran the U.S. government used its power, as explained earlier, to muscle in on a concession that had been held as a monopoly by BP since the early years of the twentieth century. Nevertheless, despite occasional tensions the governments of Great Britain and the United States along with the oil companies of the two countries have cooperated closely in the management of world oil. The negotiations for the Iranian oil that followed the Shah's return to power in 1953 clearly reveal this sort of behavior. In the negotiations, the U.S. State Department, the British Foreign Office, and seven major oil companies worked together to reach an agreement that has served as a cornerstone for further cooperation in oil. The five major U.S. oil companies were invited into the negotiations by the U.S. State Department. Before joining the talks, these five major oil companies first sought and received clearance from the attorney general concerning the antitrust implications of their cooperation in Iran. The agreement which was worked out in 1954 provided oil for all of the "seven sisters" (the major oil companies) plus some for Compagnie Française de Pétrole. British Petroleum received 40 percent of what had formerly been a monopoly, and Royal Dutch/Shell was given 14 percent. Each of the five U.S. international majors (Exxon, Socal, Mobil, Gulf, and Texaco) received 8 percent, and CFP was given 6 percent.[8] During each year, every company was permitted to take up to its share of total production at a specified price. The total production in Iran was to be determined by vote according to a formula which served to bias production downward so as to restrain world production. Cooperation between the seven majors in Iran, which was arranged under the guidance of the U.S. State Department and the British Foreign Office, strengthened the joint control over world oil exercised by the majors. By 1971 Iran had become established as the second largest oil producer in OPEC.

In 1953 the share of non-U.S. and noncommunist oil production in the hands of the seven majors was 87 percent. By 1972 that share had declined to 74 percent. In the key oil-producing states of the Middle East, however, the seven majors still held 83 percent of production in 1972. The share of the five U.S. majors alone totaled 46.7 percent of total non-U.S. noncommunist production in 1973; if we add foreign oil production by other U.S. companies in the top 20, the share of the 11 largest U.S. companies in foreign, noncommunist production was over 50 percent. The Anglo-U.S. cartel—or so-called cartel—was able to maintain its position of dominance in international oil despite a roughly sixfold increase in oil production outside of the United States and communist nations between 1953 and 1972.[9]

After World War II, the world had entered a new phase of U.S. dominance in the oil industry. The first period, in the nineteenth and early twentieth centuries, had been based on U.S. production for export. At that time, oil was much less important in the world economy than it was to become after World War II. It was used chiefly for lighting and lubrication. Use in ships as bunker fuel began before the turn of the century, but the use of oil as a fule in engines of all types was a market that was only to grow to importance later in the twentieth century.

The share of world trade in oil and oil products that was held by U.S. companies had declined with some reverses from the nineteenth century through the 1930s. The oil resources of the colonies and the large world diplomatic power of the European countries permitted their companies to eat into the U.S. share of world oil trade. But with the impact of the two world wars on relative power positions in the world, U.S. companies followed the expansion of U.S. diplomatic and military power overseas. By the 1960s, with the expanded postwar oil requirements of Western Europe and Japan, all of the noncommunist countries of the world began to find themselves dependent on U.S. oil companies for a growing share of their total energy needs. Whereas the United States' first period of dominance in world oil was based on domestic production and came during the age of coal, its second period of dominance—based on U.S. control of foreign oil supplies—saw the consumption of oil increase until oil was the most important fuel in all major industrial countries of the world.

WORLD OIL PRICES: WORLD WAR II to 1970

From the end of World War II to 1970 the cost of producing an additional barrel of oil in the Middle East was no more than about 10 to 20 cents. At the same time, the price of oil in world trade varied from over $2.00 per barrel in the late 1940s to as low as $1.20 per barrel in the late 1960s. Oil companies helped to keep the price reasonably stable and well above costs. At the same time, such prices can hardly be considered high if we look at them from several other angles.

Governments of oil-exporting countries and the oil companies are not the only groups taking a cut from the oil trade. In a 1974 article in Foreign Affairs, Jahangir Amuzegar of Iran pointed out that oil-importing countries also levy substantial taxes.

> Excise taxes alone on retail gasoline by industrial countries in 1972 ranged from a low of 32 percent in the United States to a high of 78 percent in Italy, with Japan, France, Great Britain and West Germany in the 55 to 70 percent range. In all these cases, taxes charged by consumer governments have exceeded oil producers' share per barrel of oil by more than three and one-half times. [10]

As late as 1970, the total value of petroleum exports from Saudi Arabia ($2.16 billion) was only a little more than twice the value of Brazil's coffee exports ($939 million); oil companies took a share of total export revenues for profits and to pay production costs. The prices of the 1960s were hardly fair to the oil-exporting nations and could not be considered high, even though they were at least six times production costs.

Prices on oil in international trade should be recognized as administered prices, related not to production costs but to the tax

takes of the various governments involved and the profits of the
companies. As administered prices, they reflect the wishes of the
powerful governments and company organizations involved in the oil
trade. Since World War II, European nations have not been able to
insure the security of their oil supplies (against, for example the
United States). The price increases of 1973 would have been possible
in any previous postwar year under transparent U.S. sponsorship.
at least by comparison with what has happened since 1970, world oil
prices were administered at a low level, and at several key junctures
the United States used its influence in a variety of ways to encourage
low world oil prices.

In 1948 the Marshall Plan was inaugurated to support the economic recovery of Europe, and the United States concurrently
switched to a policy of support for Japanese economic recovery.
The U.S. administrator of the Marshall Plan in Europe, Paul Hoffman, noticed that the price of oil to Europe was artificially high:
the price was determined according to the price of oil at the Gulf of
Mexico plus shipping costs to wherever the oil was to be delivered,
and this price was used whether or not the oil actually did come
from the Gulf of Mexico. Hoffman was concerned that the companies'
practice of jacking up the price of oil to Western Europe by charging
phantom freight on low-cost oil shipped from the Middle East would
cause a drag on economic recovery. At least in part on the basis of
Hoffman's protests, the companies were persuaded to institute a new
pricing plan for world oil. After 1948, prices of oil in Europe and
Japan were based on the price at the Persian Gulf plus shipping
costs. The Persian Gulf-based pricing system worked out to lower
prices on oil to Europe and Japan, along with lower profits for the
companies. The U.S. government had used its influence for the
benefit of its oil-importing allies and against the profits of its own
companies.

In 1949-50, King Ibn Saud of Saudi Arabia was pushing for
higher oil revenues from the four U.S. companies holding the Saudi
Arabian concession. The companies turned to the U.S. government,
which helped to negotiate a new agreement between Saudi Arabia and
the companies. The essence of the agreement, known as the "golden
gimmick," is that royalty payments to Saudi Arabia were trans-
formed into tax payments and increased, then, whereas the oil companies had been unable to claim deductions for their royalty payments, they were permitted to subtract their "new" foreign taxes
dollar for dollar against their U.S. tax bills. The net result was
that the Saudi government got more from the oil companies while
the U.S. government got less. The arrangement quickly spread to
other oil countries and has persisted. Over the years, U.S. taxpayers have been forced to make up the difference for billions of

dollars of tax revenues that the oil companies, under Treasury Department guidance, have redirected to the governments of the oil-exporting countries of the Middle East. To the extent that the Treasury Department's solution helped to satisfy the companies and the oil-exporting countries, it helped to keep world oil prices down. The chief beneficiaries of low world oil prices in the 1950s and 1960s were Japan and Western Europe, for the U.S. price of oil was held well above the world price from 1959 to 1973. In other words, the golden gimmick insured lower prices on oil for Europe and Japan at the expense of higher taxes in the United States. Again, the United States had used its power in oil benevolently.

In 1959 the U.S. government imposed mandatory oil import restrictions. This self-imposed, partial embargo, which raised the domestic price of oil substantially above the world price, was ostensibly designed to protect the United States from foreign control of its oil supplies. It is generally recognized that the true reason for the quota was to protect the domestic U.S. oil industry from the low price of world oil. One complementary, if unintended, effect of U.S. oil import restrictions was to weaken the demand side of the world oil market and to lower the cost of oil for Western Europe and Japan.

From 1945 to 1970, the major outlines of the story of U.S. control of world oil are clear: the U.S. government strengthened and extended the power of the major U.S. oil companies in the world cartel, using the companies as surrogates for direct colonial ownership of foreign oil. The power of the cartel was used chiefly against the oil-exporting countries to acquire low-cost supplies of oil for the companies and the oil-importing countries of Western Europe and Japan. In contrast, after 1970, the power of the cartel was turned around to squeeze profits and high prices out of the oil-importing countries for the benefit of the companies and the oil-exporting countries. But before one can understand the timing and impact of the oil price increases of the 1970s, it is necessary to realize the role of oil in the postwar industrial growth of Western Europe and Japan.

OIL AND THE U.S. PATTERN OF
INDUSTRIAL DEVELOPMENT

Throughout much of the first half of the twentieth century, the United States produced over 60 percent of the world's oil and alone accounted for about 50 percent of world consumption (see Tables 3.1 and 3.2). A unique pattern of industrial society built upon oil developed in the United States. Since World War II, the pattern of

TABLE 3.2

Consumption of Refined Petroleum Products
(1,000 bbl/day)

	1948	1962	1973	1975	Percent Change 1948-62	Percent Change 1962-73	Percent Change 1973-75
United States	5,775	10,400	17,308	16,291	80	66	-5.9
Japan	32	934	5,071	4,502	2,818	443	-11.2
West Germany	42	997	2,915	2,514	2,274	192	-13.8
Canada	228	751	1,706	1,694	229	127	-0.7
France	167	727	2,422	2,136	335	233	-11.8
United Kingdom	357	1,122	2,299	1,872	214	105	-18.6
Italy	75	669	2,147	1,853	792	221	-13.7
Soviet Bloc and China	727	3,546	8,694	8,854	388	145	+1.8
Total world	9,126	24,759	55,961	52,922	171	126	-5.4
United States and Canada as percent of world	65.8	45.0	34.0	34.0			
Japan, West Germany, France, United Kingdom, and Italy as percent of world	7.4	18.0	26.5	24.3			
Soviet Bloc and China as percent of world	8.0	14.3	15.5	16.7			

Sources: U.S. Department of the Interior, Bureau of Mines, International Petroleum Annual 1975 (Washington, D.C.: Department of the Interior, 1977), pp. 26-27; Neil H. Jacoby, Multinational Oil (New York: Macmillan, 1974), p. 55; Federal Energy Administration, Energy in Focus: Basic Data (Washington, D.C.: FEA, 1977), p. 5.

U.S. industrial society, with its heavy reliance on oil, has been adopted in Western Europe, Japan, and the Soviet Union. The former coal-based industrialized pattern, with trains, streetcars, and coal furnaces, has given way to cars, trucks, and fuel oil throughout the industrialized world. With its own supplies of oil, the United States was well placed to lead the way. Only the Soviet Union has been able to follow without heavy reliance on oil imports.

In The Stages of Economic Growth, Walt Rostow boldly sets economic history into five stages culminating in the age of high mass-consumption, Rostow's answer to the communists' classless society. It is a time when consumer durables—televisions, refrigerators, and especially cars—are made available to the masses in a society. The United States was the first nation to reach the age of high mass-consumption: by 1930 the United States had nearly one car for every five persons, while in no European country was the ratio better than one car for every 30.[11] After World War II, nations of Europe and Japan followed the U.S. pattern. Between 1949 and 1973, the number of cars, trucks, and buses in use in the world outside of the United States increased eightfold, from 17.3 million to 146.3 million.[12]

In turning to oil after World War II, Japan and the countries of Western Europe have found the benefits of cheap energy bound to the danger of energy dependence. Between 1948 and 1962, oil consumption in Japan increased by a factor of 29 (see Table 3.2). By 1962 oil imports accounted for 45 percent of Japan's total energy needs; together with a little imported coal, energy imports in 1962 for the first time came to over half of Japan's total energy needs. Thereafter, the rush to oil was headlong: by 1973, imported oil accounted for 77 percent of Japan's total energy consumption (Tables 1.1 and 3.3). In 1973 Japan was dependent on U.S. and British oil companies for 66 percent of the oil supply and for over 50 percent of its total energy.[13]

In 1925, when the United States had switched to oil and natural gas for over 25 percent of its energy, Germany was still 99 percent dependent on coal and wood. With its own coal resources, West Germany was able through most of the 1960s to keep oil and gas below 50 percent of total energy consumption (see Table 3.3). By 1970, however, low-priced oil had succeeded in displacing coal as the most important energy source, and by 1973 oil was nearly twice as important as coal for West German energy consumption. Since over 90 percent of Germany's oil must be supplied by imports, West Germany had permitted a large increase in its dependence on foreign energy in the decade before the oil crisis.

TABLE 3.3

The Switch to Oil and Gas
(percent of total energy use)

	United States		West Germany*		Japan*	
	Coal and Wood	Oil and Gas	Coal and Wood	Oil and Gas	Coal and Wood	Oil and Gas
1900	92	5	—	—	—	—
1920	80	16	—	—	—	—
1940	55	41	—	—	—	—
1950	40	56	95	4	83	6
1955	29	68	90	9	58	21
1960	23	74	76	23	46	39
1965	22	74	57	42	29	60
1970	19	77	—	—	21	72
1973	18	77	30	68	16	79

*For Japan and West Germany, values are given for selected years only.

Sources: United States: Federal Energy Agency, Energy in Focus: Basic Data (Washington, D. C.: FEA, 1977), pp. 2-3; West Germany, 1950, 1965, and 1973: Horst Mendershausen, Coping with the Oil Crisis (Washington, D. C.: Johns Hopkins Press for Resources for the Future, 1976), p. 33; West Germany, 1955 and 1960, and Japan, 1950: Joel Darmstadter, Perry Tietlebaum, and Jaroslav G. Polach, Energy in the World Economy: A Statistical Review of Trends in Output, Trade and Consumption Since 1925 (Washington, D. C.: Johns Hopkins Press for Resources for the Future, 1972), pp. 653, 655, 679; Japan, 1955-73: Yuan-li Wu, Japan's Search for Oil (Stanford: Hoover Institution Press, 1976), p. 21.

For most of the important countries of Western Europe a similar story could be told. A few Western European countries (Norway, Great Britain, the Netherlands) have discovered substantial amounts of oil and/or natural gas, but such discoveries hardly improve the access to oil and natural gas for the other European nations. In general, the countries of Western Europe have become, like Japan, heavily dependent on Middle East oil (Table 3.4). Furthermore, the condition of dependence had intensified sharply in the 1960s.

TABLE 3.4

Total Movements of Crude Oil and Petroleum Products, 1973
(thousands of barrels daily)

Exporting Countries and Regions[a]	Importing Countries and Regions[a]									
	United States	Canada	Other Western Hemisphere	Western Europe	Africa	Southeast Asia	Japan	Other Eastern Hemisphere	(Importer Unknown)	Total Exports
United States	— [b]	30	55	85	5	25	30	—	—	230
Canada	1,335	—	—	—	—	—	—	—	—	1,335
Other Western Hemisphere	2,620	500	230	355	5	5	10	—	105	3,830
Western Europe	265	—	—	—	60	—	—	10	70	405
Middle East	820	320	1,000	10,350	535	1,315	4,385	1,065	180	19,970
North Africa	360	40	175	2,545	5	—	20	265	10	3,420
West Africa	515	90	415	1,030	—	—	110	5	—	2,165
USSR and Eastern Europe	35	—	145	935	75	5	55	20	15	1,285
Other Eastern Hemisphere	255	—	—	10	—	25	1,150	45	5	1,490
Total imports	6,205	980	2,020	15,310	685	1,375	5,760	1,410	385	34,130

[a]Imports and exports reported for the various countries and regions include oil that is processed and/or transshipped.
[b]Not available.
Source: Stockholm International Peace Research Institute, Oil and Security (New York: Humanities Press, 1974), p. 71.

56

Throughout the post-World War II period, the economies of all industrialized countries have drawn together in the percentage of total energy they derive from oil and natural gas. Until 1970 the rush into oil for Japan and Western Europe was scarcely restrained by the realization that the oil resources upon which they were building a dependency were not under their control. European countries with coal industries attempted to subsidize coal production, at least partly to avoid dependence on oil, but the low price of oil throughout the 1950s and 1960s brought steadily larger shares for oil in Western Europe and Japan and led to actual declines in coal output.

In the late 1960s there was a mood of optimism about oil prices. Experts—not all, but some—were predicting oil at $1.00 per barrel. In 1971 Peter Odell commented that, "After a couple of decades of great concern over oil . . . the continent can afford to adopt a somewhat more relaxed attitude."[14]

HOW THE PRICE WENT UP IN THE 1970s

The low-price expectations of the 1960s were somehow confounded in the 1970s. Was there a real shortage as popular mythology would have us believe? Not in the physical sense: nothing could have happened in the four short years to the middle of 1973 to cause a physical shortage that would not have been perceived in the 1960s. The changes that occurred which led to the price explosion in 1973 involved increasing control by the seven major companies over flows of oil (discussed in this section) and an apparent adjustment in the attitude of the U.S. government toward high oil prices (discussed below).

In the late 1960s Libyan oil production had boomed through the Libyan government's policy of partitioning the country into a number of concessions—forcing the companies to compete in production—and letting out important concessions to companies that were not part of the world cartel. In 1969 Muammar el-Qaddafi came to power in Libya; shortly thereafter, he raised taxes on Libyan oil, severely affecting several companies whose chief source of supply was Libyan oil. The outcry over the price increase stole the spotlight from the main event: Qaddafi cut the amount of permitted production for the large independent oil companies. Libyan oil production ceased to upset markets and cartel arrangements; total Libyan production was cut back and brought into line with a program that would not upset the historical growth pattern for the rest of the oil-exporting countries of the Middle East. In the first six months of 1970, Libya had produced an average of 3.6 million barrels daily, about equal to the production of Saudi Arabia, Iran, or Venezuela.

Much of that production was in the hands of independents. By 1973 Libyan daily production had fallen to 2.2 million barrels, and by 1975 to less than 1.5 million barrels per day.[15]

In cutting oil quotas and raising taxes, Libya had violated contracts in a pattern that the U.S. State Department could have chosen to protest. Instead, as explained earlier, the U.S. government chose not to pursue the matter. The success of Libyan demands in 1970 spotlighted a serious weakness in the Anglo-U.S. cartel: company contracts with oil countries could no longer be enforced with blockades (politely known as "boycotts") as had been applied to Iran in 1951. Other countries began to push for higher oil revenues and these demands led to negotiations in Teheran in 1971. The oil companies attempted to weld the oil-exporting countries together, refusing for a time to negotiate except as a group of companies with a group of countries. In a January 15, 1971 letter from the oil companies (including the seven sisters) to the OPEC countries, the companies insisted that "we cannot further negotiate the development of claims by member countries of OPEC on any basis other than one which reaches a settlement simultaneously with all producing countries."[16]

This paradoxical behavior by the companies can be explained as an attempt to establish some contract security through the cooperation of OPEC nations in the enforcement of terms. Blockades were out; they were too blatantly a maneuver by the United States to maintain control over the oil supplies of Western Europe and Japan. If the countries, however, could be bound together in a joint contract, the companies could let the countries take public responsibility for enforcement, relying on the natural coincidence of interests between the companies and the countries to insure cooperation. If any one country attempted to charge a price for oil that was too low or to sell more oil than they were supposed to, it was in the interests of the rest of the countries as well as the cartel companies that the violator be brought into line. Any method necessary (for example, a boycott of the country's customers by the other oil-exporting countries) could be managed with legitimacy through OPEC, whereas a similar attempt at discipline fronted by the companies or their home governments would have smacked of imperialism.

Cooperation between the companies and the countries was brought closer in the early 1970s through participation by the individual oil-exporting countries in the operations of the oil companies within their borders. Meeting in Geneva in 1972, the OPEC countries proposed that all oil-exporting countries acquire partial ownership of the oil companies that were producing and selling their oil. Participation obviously involves a blending of interests. Critics of participation have often warned against the loss of company

independence: "It is not surprising . . . that participation has been
characterized as a device to restructure the oil trade so as to give
expression to producing country interests through the good offices
of the oil companies."[17] This may be putting the matter the wrong
side around; participation molded the interests of the oil-exporting
countries to those of the companies. Once the countries had partial
ownership of the companies, they had a stake in high prices and
high profits and not only in high volumes and high taxes. Production
cutbacks to preserve oil prices and profits would thereafter be in
the interests of not only the companies, but also of the countries.

With Libya brought under control, and with enhanced ability to
enforce contract decisions through OPEC, the companies were in a
position to manage much higher prices. In early 1973, only months
before the big price increases, Samuel Schurr clearly stated what
the companies' role was in price maintenance, despite participation
and OPEC involvement in price decisions.

> Oil from the Middle East and North Africa is being sold
> at a price which far exceeds its real costs of production.
> The international companies, under present and fore-
> seeable circumstances, appear to be essential to the
> continuing ability of the exporting countries to maintain
> this large margin between costs and prices.[18]

In 1973 the oil embargo and subsequent increase in the posted
price of oil—from $2.90 a barrel at the beginning of October 1973 to
$11.65 on January 1, 1974—was made in conjunction with the war
between Israel and Egypt. As a consequence, the relationship of
the two events has been debated ever since. The Arab members of
OPEC declared a total embargo of the Netherlands and the United
States for their actions with regard to Israel. Japan was later
coerced into making statements about its position on Israel to please
political leaders of oil-exporting countries. Among experts on oil,
however, a general consensus has developed that the two issues of
Israel and oil have been linked too closely in the mind of the public.
The oil crisis was brewing in any case; OPEC nations are not all
Arab; and progress on Israel is not likely to lead to large changes in
OPEC oil policies.

In 1975 the much higher prices were severely tested with a
10 percent decline in demand for OPEC oil (from 30.7 to 27.1 million
barrels daily) caused jointly by conservation and recession. The
decline in demand was met with an unprecedented cutback in supply.
According to John Blair, in his definitive book, The Control of Oil,
"the initiative for the 1975 production cutbacks came from the oil
companies."[19] Cutbacks and cartel price maintenance are the same

thing; although the oil companies leave the task of announcing prices to OPEC, the companies remain essential to the maintenance of those prices.

The task of control was made easier by a large increase in U.S. imports of oil: between 1970 and 1977, the increase in U.S. imports amounted to two-thirds of the increase in OPEC oil production, growing by 1977 to 28 percent of OPEC production.[20] Although increases in U.S. imports did not cause the price explosion, they at least made it easier for whoever controlled supplies and prices to avoid bitter disagreements over the amount of permitted production for the several nations (Table 3.6).

TABLE 3.5

Oil Prices, 1945-79
(market price, Arabian Light 34⁰,
f.o.b. Ras Tanura, Saudi Arabia)

Year*	Price ($/bbl)
1945	1.05
1947 (December)	2.22
1948 (midyear)	2.08
1949 (midyear)	1.85
1949 (end)	1.65
1960 (end)	1.50
1970	1.30
1971	1.65
1972	1.90
1973	2.70
1974	9.76
1975	10.72
1976	11.51
1977	12.40
1978	12.70
1979 (first three months)	13.34

*Prices given are average for the year unless otherwise indicated.

Sources: 1945-60: Sidney Alexander, "Background Paper," Paying for Energy, Report of the Twentieth Century Fund Task Force on the International Oil Crisis (New York: McGraw-Hill, 1975), p. 46; 1970-79: International Monetary Fund, International Financial Statistics, 30, 11 (Washington, D.C.: IMF, November 1977), p. 36; and 32, 5 (May 1979), p. 42.

TABLE 3.6

U.S. Oil Imports, 1960-78

	Total Daily Imports (million bbl)	Imports as Percentage of Demand	Percent Change from Previous Year
1960	1.8	19.8	—
1961	1.9	19.5	5.6
1962	2.1	20.3	10.5
1963	2.1	20.2	0
1964	2.3	20.9	9.5
1965	2.5	21.8	8.7
1966	2.6	21.7	4.0
1967	2.5	20.2	3.8
1968	2.8	21.2	12.0
1969	3.2	22.4	14.3
1970	3.4	23.3	6.3
1971	3.9	25.8	14.7
1972	4.7	29.0	20.5
1973	6.3	36.1	34.0
1974	6.1	36.8	3.2
1975	6.0	36.8	1.6
1976	7.3	42.0	21.6
1977	8.7	47.4	19.2
1978	8.1	43.0	6.9

Sources: Federal Energy Administration, Energy in Focus: Basic Data (Washington, D.C. FEA, 1977), p. 6; U.S. Department of Energy, Monthly Energy Review (Washington, D.C.: DOE, February 1979).

It is U.S. import behavior, as already mentioned, that is being attacked by other oil-importing nations. Complaints about U.S. oil imports should be read in part as attacks on U.S. support for high world oil prices in general, both through imports and through its oil companies. Although U.S. imports have been only a part of the story of the price increases, they are being used as symbols on which are focused dissatisfaction with the entire role of the United States in the energy crisis.

After the October war and the 1974 New Year's increase in posted oil prices to over $11 per barrel, the Western industrial nations dependent on OPEC oil were left with the task of developing a policy toward OPEC. Several of the European countries, notably France and West Germany, wanted to strengthen their bilateral relations with one or more OPEC nations. France, as the owner of CFP, a large international oil company that has been consistently frustrated in relations with the seven sisters, was able to see possible advantages for itself in probing for weaknesses in the OPEC cartel. West Germany, as a major industrial power, had more to offer than others in seeking to strengthen its bilateral relations with OPEC nations. Japan also intensified its efforts to increase economic ties with OPEC nations.

In contrast to the European attempt to pull OPEC apart through strengthened bilateral relationships, the United States attempted to keep everyone in line behind a common front in dealing with OPEC. U.S. efforts to encourage unity among the oil-importing nations were presented to the U.S. public and to the world as a move to strengthen the hand of importers against OPEC and as part of the U.S. attempt to keep Western European countries at least neutral on the matter of Israel. If one looks at the U.S. pressure from a different point of view, however, the diplomatic maneuvering of 1973 and 1974 between the major oil importers can be given another interpretation: the United States was playing its role in keeping OPEC together by preventing the major importing nations from using their economic power to set up independent ties with several individual OPEC nations. From 1971 to 1973, the oil companies, the OPEC nations, and the United States had reached a balance of advantages between themselves at the expense of the rest of the world. For the United States, it was essential that it use its influence in the consuming countries to keep them from upsetting the arrangements.

WHY THE PRICE WENT UP IN THE 1970s

While the oil companies are often castigated for their real or imagined influence for high oil prices at the expense of consumers in the oil-importing nations, critics of the oil companies have often passed too lightly over the connection between the oil companies and their home governments. As Michael Tanzer has reminded critics of the oil companies,

> One of the great myths of recent times is the notion of the "free floating" multinational corporation which roams the world like the lord of the jungle, uninfluenced by stockholders or states. . . .
> . . . the fate of the international oil companies has been and is closely tied up with the power of their

home governments, which have continually exerted
their power on behalf of the companies.[21]

The international control of oil has always been a partnership between companies and governments of home countries. Not only do
oil companies use governments, but the governments use the oil
companies as well. Considering the central importance of oil for
national security, it is safe to consider the oil companies in many
respects as servants of U.S. foreign policy—as the State Department
argued in the quote opening this chapter.

Throughout the four years from 1970, when Libya asked for
higher taxes, until the new, higher price level was achieved in 1973
the trend of events was toward a crisis, toward artificial shortages,
and toward higher world oil prices. The process of reaching that
price was attenuated in time and involved a complex of participants
acting in opposition, in support, or in conspiratorial agreement.
Negotiations between the oil companies and the oil-exporting countries were almost continuous, and the governments of the home
countries were centrally involved in these negotiations.

One key question to be answered is why the oil-price increase
occurred in the 1970s. Libyan cutbacks and so forth explain how
but not why the prices went up. Neither the oil companies nor the
oil-exporting countries had changed their position; they have always
wanted higher prices. The U.S. government did, however, find
itself in changed circumstances in the 1970s and did have reasons
to support a major price increase. Several national interests could
have contributed to U.S. government support for price increases.

Competitive Position with Japan and West Germany

As discussed in Chapter 2, the United States by the early
1970s was concerned about impending economic parity with West
Germany and Japan. If the United States could make Japan and West
Germany pay more for energy imports, perhaps the induced shortage
of energy would slow down their industrial advance. The United
States had tried to blunt the export drive of Japan and West Germany
in 1971 with the confrontation over exchange rates; it is not beyond
reason that other methods—and perhaps more effective methods—
would be attempted, if and when they became available.

The United States was concerned with the size of the economies
of Japan and West Germany and with their growing competitiveness
in industrial exports. That the United States supported higher oil
prices to benefit U.S. industry is "widely accepted in European
intellectual circles."[22] In the United States the price of oil before

1973 had been kept above the world price through the oil import quota, designed to protect the domestic U.S. oil producers. After 1973 the low controlled price on domestic crude oil in the United States was averaged in with the higher price of foreign crude and helped to keep the cost of crude oil in the United States far below the world price. Through the oil crisis, U.S. industry gained an advantage in energy prices.

The United States was concerned as well with the push into current-account surpluses by Japan and West Germany designed to finance international investment. If the oil import bills for Japan and West Germany were to be inflated by three or four times, it was a reasonable expectation that their recent trade and current-account surpluses would give way to deficits. And it is a difficult matter to finance foreign investment without foreign exchange. The U.S. grip on the economies of the world through its large volume of private direct investment would remain largely unchallenged. In 1973 the United States had $101.3 billion worth of foreign direct investment, more than 22 times the value for Japan.[23] (These are book figures and vastly understate the market value of the foreign assets.)

The Defense of U.S. Interests in Foreign Oil

U.S. efforts to expand control over the oil supplies of the Middle East and North Africa after World War II were aimed not so much at providing supervision of its own future oil supplies, which can largely be satisfied in the Western Hemisphere, but rather to establish some control over the oil supplies of Western Europe and Japan. In 1973, 61 percent of total Japanese energy requirements and 53 percent of Western European energy needs were supplied by oil imported from the Middle East and North Africa. In the same year, only 5 percent of total U.S. energy needs were supplied from the Middle East and North Africa.[24] The motive for U.S. control is apparent if one considers the often expressed fear that Western European nations might somehow become dependent on the Soviet Union for their oil supplies, either through Soviet oil exports or through Soviet success in a major Middle East oil-producing nation. However, control serves not only for defensive purposes, but also helps to maintain an element of U.S. leverage on the oil-importing nations.

The price increases of 1973 served to validate the current order, at least as far as the oil-exporting nations were concerned: with the United States as "middleman" and protector, the OPEC countries found a vast improvement in their fortunes. Oil revenues

for the governments of all OPEC countries together jumped from
$7.9 billion in 1970 to $86.6 billion in 1974. [25] High prices and
high revenues no doubt reduced the possibility that others could out-
bid for a concession or otherwise alienate an impecunious or weak
OPEC government. With higher prices the U.S. oil companies
were able to increase their profits; it is far more important, however, that the new price structure, maintained with the cooperation
of the still operative company cartel but fronted by OPEC, helped
the United States to keep its dominant position in Middle Eastern oil.

Since the new price structure has resulted in massive increases in revenue for the oil-producing states, the need for military aid has passed. Governments of the oil-exporting countries
are now able to pay for arms to defend the status quo as represented
by current governments and contracts; such governments are thereby
defending the interests of the United States.

Most of the oil exports of the OPEC nations are purchased by
countries other than the United States. Higher oil prices amount to
a self-financed military-aid program for the Middle East oil exporters and for Indonesia, Nigeria, and others. The bills for
tanks and aircraft are paid for mostly by Western Europe and Japan
in the form of higher oil prices. From the U.S. point of view, if
a massive defense buildup and an aggressive program of economic
and social development are considered necessary to make the region
stable and defensible, then higher world oil prices are much cheaper
for the United States than any program of U.S. aid. On the one
hand, Western Europe and Japan pay the bills; on the other hand,
the U.S. taxpayers would have to pay.

The Relatively Favorable Resource
Position of the United States

Aside from its relatively favorable position in oil, the United
States also produces natural gas, coal, and uranium. With both
coal and uranium, the United States completely supplies its own
needs and provides for export through domestic production. Proved
reserves of coal capable of being economically exploited are greater
than the proved reserves of all the rest of the world outside the
Soviet Union and China. From 1970 to 1975, U.S. exports of coal
to Japan contributed 3 to 6 percent (varying from year to year) of
Japan's total energy needs. The cost per ton to Japan of coal from
the United States more than doubled from 1972 to 1974. [26]

The United States has the largest reserves of uranium in the
world. With plans for the expansion of nuclear energy in the wake
of the oil crisis, the price for uranium increased from an average

of \$6.50 per pound of uranium oxide (U_3O_8) in 1973 to a spot mar-
ket price of \$42 per pound at the end of 1977.[27] Benefits to the
U.S. uranium industry have been tremendous, but the possibility
that fast-breeder technology will reduce demand for uranium fuel
remains a cloud on the horizon. President Carter's attempt to
restrict the use of fast-breeder technology around the world is
meeting resistance in West Germany and other countries, and concern for the spread of nuclear weapons is being seen in some
quarters as a front for a U.S. attempt to maintain the value of its
vast uranium reserves.[28]

The energy crisis has forced the oil-importing nations of the
world to look for alternatives. Whichever way they turn, Western
Europe and Japan find the needed raw materials in the United
States. Under the best projections about oil production throughout
this century, the world will have to increase its use of coal and of
atomic energy. Both such developments will bring a bonanza for
the United States, especially if high oil prices continue to hold up
the prices of alternative fuels.

A Note on Israel

The effect of higher oil prices upon the Arab-Israeli conflict
is complex. On the one hand, greater wealth for Arab countries
has adversely affected the position of Israel. On the other hand,
the most prominent of the newly wealthy Arab states (Saudi Arabia)
is intensely anticommunist and may speak in favor of moderation
and reconciliation in certain circumstances. None of the newly
wealthy Arab states shares a border with Israel. Certainly, the
center of gravity of the Arab world has shifted from Cairo (under
Nasser in the 1960s) to Riyadh in Saudi Arabia. This shift away
from the scene of the conflict with Israel may help to disarm local
issues in the Arab-Israeli conflict, but many other factors are
involved. The U.S. Army has a reputation for anti-Israeli feeling
and no doubt welcomes greater weapons flows to Arab states.
Other sections of the U.S. government may be more concerned
about the tilt in the balance of flows of U.S. military hardware to
the enemies of Israel. Although the relation of oil prices to the
Arab-Israeli confrontation is a murky topic, a negative conclusion
is possible; there is no reason to believe that U.S. support of
Israel is so unqualified that a policy of higher world oil prices
that would aid Arab countries and would inevitably shift U.S. attention to Arab concerns would not find support from important sectors
of the national-security establishment.

THE 1973 PRICE INCREASES IN
HISTORICAL PERSPECTIVE

After the 1973 price increases, oil alone has amounted to a
seventh of total world exports by value. But such a statistic, im-
pressive as it is, does not give a true measure of the value of oil
to the industrial nations. Oil is so important to modern industrial
society that its value must be measured in strategic and political
terms, not economic ones.

After World War II, the United States felt it was within its
interests that economic growth throughout the noncommunist world
proceed as quickly as possible. Accordingly, the United States
used its influence in world oil with restraint. In general, the joint
power of the home governments and of the companies was used to
maintain control and then to maintain low-priced oil supplies rather
than to grab large revenues from the oil-importing nations. Until
the 1970s, the power of the cartel was aimed upstream, against the
oil-exporting countries. As late as 1970, no government of any
OPEC country earned more than $1.5 billion on oil.[29]

In the early 1970s, about the time that the United States began
to feel a challenge in the economic growth of several noncommunist
industrial countries, the U.S. government began to cooperate with
attempts to raise prices by oil-exporting countries and by the oil
companies. Over a period of several years, the power of the
cartel was turned against the oil-importing countries, and a sixfold
price increase was achieved between 1971 and 1974. Since the behavior of the United States is at least questionable, surely some
response was called for by Western Europe and Japan to attempt to
hold down the price and to improve their access to energy.

NOTES

1. Anthony Sampson, The Seven Sisters: The Great Oil
Companies and the World They Made (New York: Viking Press,
1975), p. 148.
2. British Petroleum is the modern name for Anglo-Iranian
Oil Company, the company involved in Iran. In general this book
gives the modern name for oil companies in order to simplify the
presentation.
3. Sampson, p. 140.
4. James E. Atkins, "The Oil Crisis: This Time the Wolf is
Here," in The World Economic Crisis, ed. William Bundy (New
York: Norton, 1975), p. 30.

5. Neil H. Jacoby, Multinational Oil: A Study in Industrial Dynamics (New York: Macmillan, 1974), p. 26.

6. Ibid., p. 33.

7. Ibid., pp. 32, 33.

8. In order to please antitrust sentiment in the United States, each of the five U.S. majors gave 1 percent to Iricon, a consortium of smaller U.S. oil companies. In the final solution, the U.S. international majors each had 7 percent and Iricon had 5 percent. For a good explanation of the Iranian consortium, see John M. Blair, The Control of Oil (New York: Random House, 1978), pp. 43-47, 103-8.

9. Jacoby, pp. 188, 192. Jacoby concludes from the same data that during the years from 1952 to 1973, "Concentration . . . had diminished materially and by 1972 was a moderate 75 percent" (p. 189).

10. Jahangir Amuzegar, "Oil Story: Facts, Fiction and Fair Play," in Bundy, p. 72.

11. Walt Rostow, The Stages of Economic Growth: A Non-Communist Manifesto (Cambridge, England: Cambridge University Press, 1971), p. 85.

12. Jacoby, p. 52.

13. Yuan-li Wu, Japan's Search for Oil (Stanford: Hoover Institution Press, 1977), pp. 21, 26.

14. Peter Odell, Oil and World Power (Baltimore: Penguin, 1972), p. 106. Odell follows with a remarkably prescient comment:

Europe's "battle for oil" is now all over bar the
shouting except, possibly, for the period between
1971 and 1974 when the alternatives to imported
oil will not be available in large enough quantities
and thus enable the OPEC countries with international oil companies between them to squeeze
rather more money out of European consumers
(p. 107).

15. Blair, p. 228; Department of Energy (DOE), Monthly Energy Review (Washington, D.C.: DOE, January 1978), p. 86.

16. Blair, p. 224.

17. Samuel Schurr, "Minerals Trade and International Rela-tions," in The Future of the International Economic Order, ed. C. Fred Bergsten (Lexington, Mass.: Lexington, 1973), p. 192.

18. Ibid., p. 188.

19. Blair, p. 293.

20. Ibid., p. 100; DOE, pp. 8, 88; Federal Energy Admin-istration (FEA), Energy in Focus: Basic Data (Washington, D.C.: FEA), p. 6.

21. Michael Tanzer, The Energy Crisis: World Struggle for Power and Wealth (New York: Monthly Review Press, 1974), p. 38.

22. Blair, p. 295.

23. U.S. Department of Commerce, Bureau of the Census, Statistical Abstract of the United States 1978 (Washington, D. C.: Department of Commerce, 1978), p. 864; Sueo Sekiguchi, "Japan on the Threshold of Becoming a Capital Exporter," Wall Street Journal, March 23, 1978.

24. For West Germany and Japan: Stockholm International Peace Research Institute (SIPRI), Oil and Security (New York: Humanities Press, 1974), p. 14. For the United States, petroleum, including natural gas liquids, provided 47 percent of total U.S. energy; 36 percent of petroleum came from imports; and 29 percent of U.S. oil imports came directly or indirectly from the Middle East and North Africa: .36 x .47 x .29 = .05. Data for the United States: DOE, p. 3; FEA, pp. 8, 10.

25. SIPRI, p. 40.

26. Yoshie Yonezawa, "Resource Trade and Economic Security: The Case of Coal," in Australian-Japanese Economic Relations in Context: Recent Experiences and the Prospects Ahead, ed. Peter Drysdale and Kiyoshi Kojima (Canberra: Australian National University Press, 1972), pp. 80, 82; Wu, p. 21.

27. U.S. Department of the Interior, Bureau of Mines, Mineral Commodity Summaries 1978 (Washington, D. C.: Government Printing Office, 1978), p. 182.

28. See, for example, Daniel Yergin, "For Better or Worse, Nuclear Power is Europe's Best Bet," Baltimore Sunday Sun, May 7, 1978, p. K2.

29. SIPRI, p. 40.

4

INTERNATIONAL ECONOMICS AFTER 1973: SURPLUSES AND DEFICITS

> What we are witnessing today in the field of inter-
> national economic relations—in the monetary field
> and now in the field of oil and raw material prices—
> is . . . a struggle for the world product.
> Helmut Schmidt, 1974[1]

The oil-price increases in the 1970s have amounted to an oil tax of about 1.5 to 3 percent of GNP for most of the oil-importing countries of the world. Nevertheless, it has not been the inability of nations to pay but rather the willingness and insistence of the major nations to pay for oil in current exports, instead of through borrowing, that has created the biggest problems for the world economy since 1973. In other words, it has not been the cost of oil that has created the problems, but almost exactly the opposite: nations have wished to export more and to pay the increased cost of oil immediately instead of borrowing and paying the higher prices with an increase in debt.

From 1973 to 1977, OPEC nations spent considerably less on imports than they were earning on exports. This meant that other nations wishing to pay for oil found—in the aggregate—that they could not pay the whole bill and had to borrow as well. Competition between nations for the limited market, in order to avoid the need to borrow, caused severe problems. The struggle to determine who could sell and who had to borrow is known of as the "problem of adjustment" to the oil-price increases. In other words, adjustment was not difficult in a theoretical or an economic sense; the struggle to adjust had nothing to do with stupidity or poverty. The basis of the adjustment problem was the deliberate and measured use of national power by the three major noncommunist industrial powers to achieve certain nationalistically defined ends.

By 1978 and 1979, large increases in OPEC imports had solved the problem of paying for oil. Nevertheless, the fight for trade surpluses and market shares continues among the big three industrial nations. How and why Japan and West Germany have run trade and current-account surpluses after 1973 in spite of higher oil import bills are key questions that must be answered by anyone who tries to explain the post-1973 course of the world economy. Those questions, along with other matters, are the subjects of this chapter.

BALANCING THE OPEC SURPLUSES

A Zero-Sum Game

A zero-sum game is one in which the gains of one are matched by the losses of another. Cutting up a pie is a zero-sum game: if one person gets a larger piece, then another must get a smaller. A private game of poker is a zero-sum game: if one person wins $100, then everybody else together must lose $100. International trade is, in some respects, a zero-sum game. What one country exports another must import. Therefore, if one country runs a trade surplus— exports more than it imports—other countries together must run a deficit—import more than they export. The sum of all trade deficits and trade surpluses in the world will theoretically be identical to zero.[2]

In a zero-sum game, an effort for private gain could be seen as an effort to pin a loss on somebody else; there is no way that all can gain together. Similarly, in international trade, the effort of any one nation to increase exports or to decrease imports has a direct if unintended effect on other nations. From the point of view of the common good, the best one can hope for in world trade patterns is a sustainable and stable pattern of deficits and surpluses that are acceptable if not inevitable for the participants.

Before going further, the concept of the trade balance must be replaced in the present discussion with the concept of the current-account balance. In talking about how well nations are able to pay for oil, the current-account balance is more appropriate because it includes all current international income and expenses for a nation. The trade balance includes only net income on merchandise trade. Nations receive additional income on services sold to nonresidents (for example, patent rights and tourist services; income on foreign investment is treated as income on the sale of a service). And some income is received as gifts from nonresidents: foreign aid, private foundation grants, or remittances of wages or pensions from a foreign country. Similarly, purchases of services and gifts to nonresidents are items of current expenditure. For a nation, the total of all receipts and expenses on current account indicates how well it is able to operate on a "pay as you go" basis.

Deficits or surpluses on current account seldom exceed 1 or 2 percent of GNP for large industrial nations or 5 percent of GNP for small industrialized and less developed countries. The limit is set by the ability and willingness of nations to go into deficit. A deficit nation—like a family living beyond its means—may find benefits for itself by going into debt. In borrowing money to buy foreign goods a deficit nation is able to increase its consumption and investment in the present against a promise to pay in the future.

For most industrialized countries, there are strong internal political restraints against running current-account deficits. Farmers, industrialists, and union leaders in the developed nations are nearly unanimous in opposition to any policy of cheap and plentiful imports, such as would be implied by consistently large current-account deficits. Any government of an industrialized nation that ignored the desires of such pressure groups would soon find itself with political difficulties.

If a deficit nation does not itself find its own limits, then its creditors—banks, other governments, or the International Monetary Fund—may step in to force a change in its economic policies in order to restrain the size of its deficits. This is most often true for the less developed countries, which characteristically have industrial, union, and farm pressure groups that are too weak to restrain the interests of the urban bureaucratic class for more and cheaper imported food and other consumer goods.

Just as some nations will accept deficits, others find that their national interests are better served by surpluses. A nation in surplus is working in one way or another to increase its influence over other nations. For most of the period since World War II, only the United States has been able to run consistently large current-account surpluses. Such surpluses have been a privilege of industrial preeminence and world power, so there was not too much that anybody else could do about the matter in any case. Only since the late 1960s has the United States experienced any competition from other nations seeking large current-account surpluses.

Although deficit nations can be disciplined by their creditors, nations with large surpluses are more difficult to deal with, for they come knocking as salespersons rather than as indigents seeking loans. If the sum of all desired surpluses exceeds the deficits that others will accept, then at least one nation will find itself disappointed. How to apportion surpluses among the large industrial nations and how to coerce a surplus nation (such as Japan in the 1970s) to restrain its current-account surpluses are problems that underlie all the economic summitry of the late 1970s.

Throughout the 1950s and most of the 1960s, the zero-sum game of international current account balances was played according to "Captain, may I?" rules; with its military umbrella over the West, and with its lead in most high-technology manufactures, the United States played the role of captain. In general, the United States played its role with benevolence (or with enlightened self-interest), running current-account surpluses but effectively promoting stability in international trade and supporting economic growth and export expansion wherever possible; between 1953 and 1973, the volume of world exports grew 8 percent per year on the average compared to a 5 percent growth rate for world output.[3] In the late 1960s and early 1970s, with the declining U.S. share of exports in world trade, and especially in manufactures, the United States lost its captaincy as well as its good will toward other industrial nations of the free world. For their part, Japan and West Germany were no longer content to run deficits or modest surpluses, and with their push into substantial surpluses the United States found itself in a struggle in which it was no longer able to control the situation. The game took on the character of a battle royal. It is still a zero-sum game, but there is yet no new basis for cooperation and stability equivalent to that provided by U.S. leadership in the 1950s and 1960s.

The 1973 oil-price increases had a further shattering effect on international trade patterns, rules, and practices. Since 1973, the income of the oil-exporting countries has been swollen by the higher oil prices, but not all the additional income has been spent on imports of goods and services or given away in aid. Since 1973, surpluses on current account for all OPEC nations together have been as high as $64.7 billion in 1974, dipped below $30 billion in 1977,[4] and then dropped to an estimated $11 billion in 1978. The monstrous surpluses of 1974-76 were larger than anything that had been experienced to that time. From 1971 to 1973, aggregate surpluses for all the surplus nations in the world had totaled an average of only $15 billion. Post-1973 surpluses in the OPEC nations gave a new twist to the zero-sum game of current-account deficits and surpluses: for several years one group of players regularly "won" a $30-40 billion surplus no matter what the other players did. That left $30-40 billion in deficits to be shared among other nations. Any nation that had a current-account balance merely increased the share of the deficit for the rest, and a non-OPEC nation with a current-account surplus was outstandingly uncooperative, not only refusing to share the deficits but actually serving to increase the total burden of deficits for other nations.

The struggle over the location of deficits during 1974-77 was acrimonious for several related reasons. First, the United States was no longer able to "arm twist" and to bully Japan and West

Germany into cooperative deficits. Second, the conditions for stability—substantial deficits year after year—were onerous and unpalatable for Japan and West Germany in their modern drive for world economic power. By 1978, with the OPEC current-account surplus down to $11 billion, the matter of placing the balancing deficits had ceased to be a problem. Among the big three, however, large U.S. deficits and large Japanese and West German surpluses in 1977 and 1978 revealed a continuing struggle for market shares in the world.

The Preferred Solution and the Behavior
of the Big Three

The need for current-account deficits to balance OPEC surpluses was immediately realized by economic planners in the major oil-importing countries. As early as January 1974, only weeks after the posted price of oil had jumped from $5.11 to $11.65 per barrel, the major nations (in the Rome Communiqué of the "Committee of Twenty" of the International Monetary Fund) collectively stated their understanding that a large, aggregate current-account deficit was inevitable for non-OPEC nations and urged that each nation accept its share of the deficit. During the following month leaders of European nations, Japan, and the United States met at the Washington Energy Conference; the final communiqué shows they had again discussed the matter of balancing deficits: "In dealing with the balance of payments impact of oil prices they stressed the importance of avoiding competitive depreciation and the escalation of restrictions on trade."[5]

In a late March 1974 meeting of economists from the Brookings Institution, the Japanese Economic Research Center, and the European Community Institute for University Studies, the problem of balancing deficits was dealt with in simple and clear terms: "The current account surpluses of the petroleum exporting countries necessarily imply deficits for the rest of the world." The economists went on to consider the possibility that "nations . . . might try to resist the deterioration in their current account positions arising from higher oil import costs by cutting back on other imports or by expanding their exports." But such a policy on the part of any one nation would not be in the interests of the group.

> Any marked improvement in the ability of one of the oil importing nations to finance its oil-induced current account deficit, through higher exports or reduced non-oil imports, will come at the expense primarily of a further deterioration in the current accounts of other [nations].[6]

In 1974 the Minister of Finance and soon-to-be Chancellor of West Germany, Helmut Schmidt, delivered a parallel interpretation, warning that

> it would be a great mistake if each individual country within the group of oil consumers were now selfishly to try to solve its payments and employment problems by pursuing beggar-my-neighbor policies at the expense of its trading partners. [7]

Economists very early came up with recommended schemes to make explicit each nation's share of the oil deficits to balance OPEC surpluses. Two such recommendations are given by Sidney Alexander in a study sponsored by the Twentieth Century Fund and published in 1975. One of the systems Alexander described for allocating the balancing deficits for OPEC surpluses is based on the volume of oil imports.

> Suppose . . . that in 1975 the OPEC surplus is $45 billion and OPEC oil exports are 27 m.b.d. [million barrels per day]. Then the proportional current account target for each oil importing nation would be a deficit of $1.67 billion per m.b.d. of oil imported ($45 billion divided by 27 m.b.d.). [8]

The second system Alexander described for allocating shares of the balancing deficits is based on where OPEC invests its foreign earnings. For example,

> if . . . the OPEC countries invested $4 billion of the projected $45 billion surplus in the United States in 1975, then the United States . . . target for the year would be a $4 billion current-account deficit. [9]

Economists and officials in the major oil-consuming countries clearly recognized that the non-OPEC nations had to run collective deficits to offset OPEC surpluses. In 1974 they stated repeatedly their joint understanding that it was against the common interest for any one nation to attempt to shift its oil deficit onto others by shutting out imports or pushing its exports. Furthermore, there were formulas readily available that would help to determine the appropriate amount of deficits to be accepted by any nation. But despite the clear understanding and pious pronouncements of concern for the common good, the behavior of the major industrial powers since 1973 has been totally at odds with the behavior they jointly advocated.

From 1973 to 1978 the three largest noncommunist industrial powers have jointly imported an amount of oil equivalent to about a half of total OPEC oil exports.[10] Their aggregate oil-import bill has jumped from an average of $10 billion annually for 1970-72 to $58 billion in 1974 and to $82 billion by 1977 (see Table 4.1). Nevertheless, if we look at the aggregate current-account balance of the big three, it was in surplus for all three years from 1974 to 1976, and in each of the three years from 1974 to 1976 the aggregate surplus was larger than it had been in any of the three years from 1970 to 1972.

Taken collectively, the big three were able through the years 1974 to 1976 to pay all of the increased cost of their oil imports through improvements in their trade surplus with the rest of the world. From 1973 to 1974, for example, West Germany paid $7 billion more for oil but increased its merchandise export proceeds by $22 billion against a $9-billion increase in non-oil merchandise imports. Not only did the big three not take a share of deficits to balance OPEC surpluses, they actually added onto the deficits of others by increasing the size of their own surpluses.

The plan to share oil deficits apparently never won the resolve of the big three (aside from Japan, perhaps, which ran current-account deficits for several years after the oil price increase). What was happening was very quickly picked up by economists who looked at the data. In his study of the economic aspects of the oil crisis, Alexander noted that

> The OECD countries [chiefly Western Europe, Japan, and the United States] have pledged to avoid competitive devaluations and trade restraints. Nevertheless, many of them have been attempting to reduce their deficits, principally by stimulating exports but also by domestic demand management aimed at reducing imports . . . the policies these countries adopted in 1974 and 1975 did not recognize deficits consistently. Country after country tried to eliminate its deficits—by approved means, of course.[11]

In a June 1977 confidential report on the world economy by the staff of the International Monetary Fund, the current-account performance of the big three was noted in much the same terms.

> In these three countries, oil-related deficits were rapidly offset by positive changes . . . elsewhere in the current account. Inevitably, these big shifts . . . put strong downward pressure on the current account

TABLE 4.1

Selected Trade Statistics for the "Big Three," 1970–78
($ millions)

	1970	1971	1972	1973	1974	1975	1976	1977	1978
United States									
Current-account balance	2,383	-1,410	-5,989	6,881	1,220	18,456	4,339	-15,276	-15,958
Merchandise trade balance	2,603	-2,267	-6,418	913	-5,338	9,051	-9,353	-31,125	-34,147
Oil-import bill	2,764	3,323	4,300	7,674	24,329	25,027	31,390	41,026	38,560
West Germany									
Current-account balance	848	875	747	4,371	9,804	4,059	3,902	3,799	8,824
Merchandise trade balance	5,691	6,383	8,360	15,337	22,173	17,677	16,689	19,400	25,150
Oil-import bill	2,201	3,200	3,333	5,620	12,431	11,770	13,980	14,816	16,066
Japan									
Current-account balance	1,970	5,797	6,624	-136	-4,693	-682	3,680	10,911	16,599
Merchandise trade balance	3,963	7,787	8,971	3,694	1,456	5,073	9,943	17,312	24,723
Oil-import bill	2,700[a]	3,622	4,477	6,725	21,162	20,994	23,284	25,783	25,676
Total									
Current-account balance	5,201	5,262	1,382	11,116	6,331	21,833	11,921	-566	9,465
Merchandise trade balance	12,257	11,883	10,913	19,944	18,291	31,801	17,459	5,587	15,726
Oil-import bill	7,665	10,145	12,110	20,019	57,922	57,791	68,654	81,625	80,302
OPEC current-account surplus	1,000	3,000	3,000	5,700	64,700	30,400	36,300	29,500	—[b]

[a]Estimated: The value of Japan's crude oil imports in 1970 was 75.5 percent of the value in 1971; assuming that this same relationship holds true for all petroleum imports, we get an estimate for Japan's 1970 petroleum import bill as .755 x 3,622 = 2,735, which may be rounded off to 2,700.

[b]Not available.

Sources: United States, Japan, and West Germany: International Monetary Fund, International Financial Statistics, 30, 11 (Washington, D.C.: IMF, November 1977), pp. 148-51, 204-7, 368-71; IFS, 30, 5 (May 1977), pp. 236-37; IFS, 31, 12 (December 1978), pp. 152-55, 208-11, 386-89; IFS, 32, 5 (May 1979), pp. 154-57, 212-15, 388-91; IFS, 32, 6 (June 1979), p. 156; OPEC: Citibank, Economics Department, "OPEC Spends Its Way to Growth," Economic Week (October 16, 1978); Testimony of David T. Devlin, in U.S. Congress, Senate, Committee on Banking, Housing and Urban Affairs, Economic and Financial Impact of OPEC Oil Prices, 95th Cong., 1st sess., January 5, 1977, p. 48.

position of other oil importing countries, whose combined current account balance shifted from a deficit
of $7 billion in 1973 to one of $55 billion in 1976.[12]

The IMF staff nevertheless opined that the improvements they
noted in the current-account positions of the big three were "not an
objective of policies," but were rather accidental results of anti-
inflation policies and so forth.[13] Such an assessment seems more
diplomatic than incisive.

If we compare the events of the period from 1970 to 1972 with
what happened after 1973, there has clearly been a large improvement in the current account position of the big three relative to
other non-OPEC countries. Much of the explanation for this improvement can be found in the same process which broke up the
system of multilaterally approved exchange rates in 1971: the big
three were fighting among themselves for markets in the world.
From 1971 to 1973 was a period of drastic devaluation for the U.S.
dollar. As the value of the dollar fell, U.S. goods were made
cheaper in world markets. The U.S. trade and current-account
balances began to show improvement in 1973 and continued an im-
pressive improvement through 1975. In the face of the U.S. effort
to regain its market position, West Germany more than held its
own throughout, while Japan's trade and current-account balances
suffered badly in 1973 (before the oil-price increases) and 1974,
but improved more or less steadily from 1975 through 1978.

With the U.S. plunge into deficits in 1977 and 1978, the big
three as a group began to behave a little bit more reasonably in historical terms, accepting a $5-billion deterioration in their aggre-
gate current-account balance in 1977 relative to the 1970-72 average. (Over the same period, the aggregate oil-import bill had increased by about $72 billion.) But such aggregate figures mask the
shift in current-account positions among the big three: the United
States had a current-account deficit of $15 billion in 1977; Japan in
that year ran a surplus of $11 billion; and West Germany had a sur-
plus of $4 billion. In 1977, the U.S. current-account position was
thus $30 billion less than that of Japan and West Germany combined,
and the situation worsened in 1978. By comparison, the U.S.
current-account balance in 1970 and 1971 was an average of $2 bil-
lion less than that of West Germany and Japan combined, and the
situation at that time was so bad in the eyes of U.S. planners that
the United States deliberately broke up the Bretton Woods system
of multilateral agreement on exchange rates in order to improve
the U.S. trade balance.

If we look at the merchandise trade balance, the difficulties
besetting the United States in the world economy are even more

clearly delineated. The U.S. trade balance exceeded that of Japan and West Germany together in all but one year from World War II through 1965. By 1970-71 the U.S. trade balance averaged $12 billion less than that of Japan and West Germany combined and in 1977 was $68 billion less. Through the 1970s, and through the oil crisis, the struggle by Japan and West Germany to increase their economic power and influence in the world had continued. It was a struggle which necessarily brought them into conflict with the United States; the trade and current-account balances of the United States continued to suffer while those of Japan and West Germany showed larger and larger surpluses.

Deficits for Others

From 1974 to 1976 the big three made it very difficult for other nations by pushing their share of the balancing deficits onto their trading partners. Table 4.2 illustrates the global allocation of deficits and surpluses by groups of countries. Continuing surpluses in some developed countries (chiefly the United States and West Germany) left larger deficits for other countries, both developed and less developed. The allocation of deficits among specific countries is more clearly illustrated in Table 4.3, which lists non-OPEC countries that have been particularly significant in the distribution of deficits after 1973. Those nations that took more than their share of balancing deficits have been characterized by Paul Watson in an Overseas Development Council study as

> the "poor rich" and the "rich poor" nations, the former including the severely troubled European nations, such as the United Kingdom and Italy, as well as their less-industrialized Mediterranean neighbors, and the latter encompassing mainly the higher-income developing nations such as Brazil, Mexico.[14]

Only 27 nations accounted for a deficit shift of over $50 billion between 1970-73 and 1974-76. This shift exceeded the OPEC shift into surplus (see Tables 4.2 and 4.3). Other nations with smaller deficit shifts are not listed. In every year since 1973 (except 1975) Western European nations, together with Australia, New Zealand, and Canada, have taken more of the balancing deficits than have the non-oil less developed countries.

In 1977 U.S. deficits on current account turned the surpluses of the big three as a group into deficits despite Japan's turnaround from large deficits to large surpluses. From 1975 to 1977, the U.S.

TABLE 4.2

World Distribution of Current-Account Deficits
and Surpluses, 1971-76
($ billions)

	Average 1971-73	Average 1974-76
Surplus countries		
OPEC[a]	2.8	49.0
OECD[b]	12.3	15.3
Total	+15.1	+64.3
Deficit countries		
OPEC	-1.4	-2.0
OECD	-6.7	-37.0
Less developed countries	-4.1	-23.0
Other[c]	-2.7	-12.3
Total	-14.9	-74.6
Residual[d]	-0.2	+10.3

[a]OPEC countries: Algeria, Ecuador, Gabon, Indonesia, Iran, Iraq, Kuwait, Libya, Nigeria, Qatar, Saudi Arabia, United Arab Emirates, Venezuela.

[b]OECD countries: United States, Japan, West Germany, France, Great Britain, Canada, Italy, Australia, New Zealand, Austria, Belgium, Denmark, Finland, Greece, Iceland, Ireland, Luxembourg, Netherlands, Norway, Portugal, Spain, Sweden, Switzerland, Turkey.

[c]Other: Israel, South Africa, nonmarket economies of Eastern Europe, the Soviet Union, and China.

[d]The positive residual for 1974-76 is attributed by the International Monetary Fund to overreporting of service imports and underreporting of service exports.

Source: National Advisory Council on International Monetary and Financial Policies, "Special Report on U.S. Participation in the Supplementary Financing Facility," in U.S. Congress, House, Committee on Banking, Finance and Urban Affairs, Subcommittee on International Trade, Investment and Monetary Policy, U.S. Participation in the Supplementary Financing Facility of the International Monetary Fund, 95th Cong., 1st sess., September 1977, p. 101.

TABLE 4.3

Countries with Large Deteriorations in Their Current-Account
Balances from 1970 to 1976
($ billions)

	Average 1970–73	Average 1974–76	Average[a] 1977–78	Change from 1970–73 to 1974–76	Change from 1974–76 to 1977–78
OECD countries					
United Kingdom	0.745	-4.683	-0.186	-5.428	4.497
Italy	0.675	-3.803	1.669[b]	-4.478	5.472
Spain	0.514	-3.742	-1.205[c]	-4.256	2.537
France	0.108	-3.993	-2.015[b]	-4.101	1.978
Canada	0.303	-3.598	-4.345	-3.901	-0.747
Norway	-0.298	-2.434	-4.225[b]	-2.136	-1.791
Sweden	0.358	-1.420	-3.376	-1.778	-1.956
Turkey	0.173	-1.458	-2.225	-1.631	-0.767
Australia	-0.162	-1.531	-2.948	-1.369	-1.417
Portugal	0.348[d]	-0.958	-1.641	-1.296	-0.683
Finland	-0.272	-1.522	0.038	-1.250	1.560
Denmark	-0.374	-1.126	-1.364	-0.752	-0.238
New Zealand	-0.207	-0.849	-0.384	-0.642	0.465
Austria	-0.161	-0.759	-2.201	-0.598	-1.442
Belgium	0.964	0.436	-0.573	-0.528	-1.009
Greece	-0.590	-1.108	-1.516	-0.518	-0.403
Less developed countries					
Brazil	-1.282	-6.716	-5.681	-5.434	1.035
Mexico	-1.063	-3.485	-1.489	-2.422	1.996
Pakistan	-0.365	-1.813	-0.674[b]	-1.448	1.139
Peru	-0.031	-1.152	-0.834	-1.121	0.318
Korea	-0.537	-1.442	-0.343	-0.905	1.099
Philippines	-0.126	-0.732	-0.829[c]	-0.858	-0.097
Taiwan	-0.313	-0.436	1.235	-0.749	1.671
Egypt	-0.144	-0.844	-0.814[b]	-0.700	0.030
Others					
South Africa	-0.718	-1.971	1.087	-1.253	3.058
Israel	-0.391	-1.636	-0.698[b]	-1.245	0.938
Yugoslavia	-0.048	-1.111[e]	-1.602[c]	-1.063	-0.491
Total				-51.860	15.653

[a]For 1977 through the second quarter of 1978, unless otherwise indicated.
[b]1977 and first quarter of 1978.
[c]1977 only.
[d]1972-73 only.
[e]1974-75 only.

Source: International Monetary Fund, International Financial Statistics 30, 11 (Washington, D.C.: IMF, November 1977), and 31, 12 (December 1978).

current-account balance had declined by $34 billion. With the U.S. deficits and the declining surpluses of the OPEC countries in 1977 and 1978, current-account balances in other countries were able to show some improvement. By 1977-78, the aggregate current-account deficits for countries outside of OPEC and outside of the big three were not far out of line with historical experience in terms of the percent of total world exports represented by the deficits. Thus, the problem of adjustment to OPEC surpluses had merged into the old issue of declining U.S. fortunes relative to Japan and West Germany. The United States had been unable to persuade Japan or West Germany to cooperate in sharing deficits.

The period from 1974 to 1976 had presented foreign-trade and payments problems to Italy, the United Kingdom, and other nations. By 1977-78, the United States, through a large increase in its trade deficit, had helped to pull the most severely affected countries away from the danger of having to put strict controls on foreign trade. The multilateral trade system was more secure in that respect, but the serious deterioration of U.S. current-account and trade balances against those of West Germany and Japan represented a problem that was of longer standing and promised to be more difficult. The main issue for economic adjustment to the oil crisis was the ability of the big three to cooperate. From 1974 to 1976, the United States and West Germany had fought for surpluses. By 1977-78, the United States had given up its surpluses to help maintain the multilateral trading system, but Japan and West Germany had continued to push for surpluses and showed no willingness to cooperate with the United States. Insofar as cooperation among the big three is the sine qua non of a successful international economic order, their inability to compromise and share the deficits was evidence of a failing system. Although by 1978 and 1979 the OPEC surpluses had decreased to the point that the issue of placing deficits to balance OPEC surpluses was a matter of the past, continued large U.S. deficits in the face of Japanese and West German surpluses promise more difficulties in later years.

THE HOW AND WHY OF JAPANESE AND
WEST GERMAN CURRENT-ACCOUNT SURPLUSES

During 1977 U.S. foreign economic policy makers spent a lot of time on Capitol Hill explaining to Congress the disposition of the world economy and the rationale behind various U.S. policies. In a hearing before the Senate Subcommittee on Foreign Economic Policy, the Under Secretary for Economic Affairs of the Department of State, Richard Cooper, had a difficult time persuading Senator Frank Church of the wisdom of U.S. deficits in the face of Japanese and West German surpluses.

> MR. COOPER: . . . In the aggregate, the current account deficits in stronger economies are greatly important to the smooth function of the monetary system, insofar as they represent imports other than oil.
>
> SEN. CHURCH: At that point, one of these strong economies, usually the German, Japanese, and Americans, are mentioned in that category. What strong economy is operating in a deficit position other than our own?
>
> MR. COOPER: Of course, by size, the United States is, far and away, the biggest economy. We are now in substantial deficit. After that come Japan and Germany respectively, both of which countries are in surplus. Japan in substantial surplus.
>
> SEN. CHURCH: These are the only one of these economies operating according to doctrine?
>
> MR. COOPER: . . . Of the big three, the United States is the only one running a deficit. . . .
>
> SEN. CHURCH: What happens to the doctrine if nobody heeds it?
>
> MR. COOPER: The most important country is heeding it.
>
> SEN. CHURCH: The United States, important as it may be, cannot rectify the problem worldwide without very substantial assistance from other countries. You are not suggesting that we just shoulder the whole load ourselves, even though the world is off in another direction?
>
> MR. COOPER: We are not talking about the world; we are talking about two other countries. I am not suggesting or urging—
>
> SEN. CHURCH: You are talking about the world, very definitely. The two other countries are the two other major strong economies. They are not conforming to our doctrine. We are pretty much alone. What is the use of a doctrine if it is ignored by the economies that are supposed to follow our lead?[15]

The failure of the United States to enlist Japanese and West German cooperation in taking a share of the large 1974-77 deficits to balance OPEC surpluses was an oft-repeated theme in the U.S. government's deliberations on the world economy. Professor Aliber, testifying before a House subcommittee in 1977, stated succinctly, "We have been unsuccessful in getting the Germans and the Japanese to share in those deficits."[16] As early as June 1976 in hearings before the same subcommittee, C. Fred Bergsten had made much the same point about Japanese and West German surpluses.

> [The president] should press the other surplus countries, notably Japan and Germany, to expand their economies more vigorously, and/or let their exchange rates rise in value. The United States has set an exemplary trend in that area, a stellar example, while leading the recovery of the world economy and moving into temporary trade deficit, thus supporting the recoveries of others.[17]

The current-account surpluses of Japan and West Germany are bothersome to the United States; from 1974 to 1977, they seemed out of phase with the need for deficits to balance OPEC surpluses; and they seem curious in the light of the much higher oil-import bills for Japan and West Germany. How and why do Japan and West Germany continue to run current-account surpluses?

Japanese and West German Surpluses: How?

In order to buy West German goods, whether one is German, Czech, or French, one has to pay, ultimately, in marks. Thus, for West Germany to run a surplus involves making more deutsche marks available to foreigners than West Germany is paying to foreigners in buying their goods. For example, in 1976 West Germany sold as exports $124 billion in goods and services but imported only $113 billion in goods and services. In purchasing these goods and services in world markets, West German residents exchanged 280 billion DM for foreign currencies; net transfers (gifts) to foreigners came to another 18 billion DM. But in buying $124 billion worth of West German goods and services, residents of other countries needed 312 billion DM. Much of the difference was made up through the exchange of DM for dollars by the German central bank. In 1976, the West German central bank purchased a net total of $4 billion, investing the purchased dollars mostly in short-term (and some long-term) U.S. government debt. The deutsche marks that the West German central bank made available in the exchange of deutsche marks for dollars more or less had to be used for the purchase of West German goods for export, since the West German government refused to let foreigners invest in mark-denominated bonds with less than two years remaining maturity and also controlled interest

payments on mark-denominated bank deposits belonging to foreigners. Those are the sorts of assets that the West German central
bank bought with its accumulated dollars, and they are the sorts of
assets that foreign investors interested in holding deutsche marks
would want to buy.

The details are messy but the intent is clear: West Germany
was trying to make marks available for foreigners, but only for the
purchase of West German goods. In a July 1977 Bundesbank (West
German central bank) report, the reason for controls on inflows of
short-term funds was given as a desire to avoid the deutsche mark's
being put in the role of a reserve currency.[18] In other language,
this means that the Bundesbank wants to hold down the value of the
deutsche mark, to force foreigners to buy West German goods with
any marks they have on hand, and thus to insure a trade surplus. If
the mark were made available as a reserve currency (that is, if foreigners were permitted to invest in short-term, liquid, mark-
denominated assets) then the Bundesbank would lose control over
the West German trade surplus and over the value of the deutsche
mark. On the other hand, the West German central bank was taking
the dollars it had purchased and was investing them instead of making them available for West Germans to purchase foreign goods as
imports. In short, the West German surplus in 1976 can be explained neatly and completely through the dollar-buying and -invest-
ing program of the West German central bank and by controls that
prevented foreigners from investing deutsche marks in short-term
liquid assets.

An equivalent argument holds to explain the surpluses of Japan.
The central banks of both countries have been buying dollars and investing them in U.S. government liabilities. The governments of
both countries block an equivalent inflow of short-term investment
through controls on the sorts of assets foreigners may hold. From
1975 to 1977, West Germany ran a cumulative current-account surplus of $12 billion. In the same three years, holdings of U.S. gov-
ernment debt by the West German central bank increased by $6 bil-
lion. For Japan, much of the cumulative surplus of $16 billion in
1976 and 1977 was made possible through a $9-billion increase in
Japanese central bank holdings of U.S. government debt.

Aside from selling goods for cash, all major trading nations
make their goods available on credit, often through various sorts
of government loan programs. Such credit programs are channels
through which, for example, Japan or West Germany can make their
currencies and goods available directly to foreigners without the
foreigners having to trade foreign exchange for yen or deutsche
marks. For example, a Philippine importer may borrow one billion
yen, purchase Japanese goods for export to the Philippines, and be
left with a loan payable to Japanese banks or to the government.[19]

For Japan in particular, official export credit and insurance programs have been very important. In 1976, a report by the staff of the House Subcommittee on International Trade, Investment and Monetary Policy assessed the Japanese export credit and insurance program as "highly competitive with those of the other major trading nations," and noted that "About 47 percent of total Japanese exports benefitted from official support in 1975." In the same report the staff noted that for West Germany, ". . . the degree of support provided under official German export programs is rather modest." In 1975, only 7 percent of West German exports were benefited by official programs. For the United States, the equivalent 1975 figure was 12 percent. Thus, it appears that of the big three Japan relies the most on its export credit and insurance program to make its currency and its goods available to foreign customers.[20]

Policies to manipulate exchange rates, such as central bank purchases of dollars, controls on the sorts of assets foreigners may acquire, and government support for exports and export credit, are recognized in some circles—and especially in high government and financial circles—as the keys to continuing surpluses in Japan and West Germany. The usual construction of the argument is that for Japan, for example, to buy dollars holds up the price of the dollar and holds down the price of the yen, while Japan's restriction of foreign investment in certain yen assets holds down demand for yen and thus also helps to keep down the value of the yen. A low-priced yen promotes exports of Japanese goods. Thus, by a more circuitous argument we get the same result: government intervention in foreign exchange markets can be used to promote a current-account surplus.

In 1976, Bergsten commented in testimony before a House subcommittee,

> Japan is likely to run the largest rate surplus in its history this year, yet it has been buying dollars massively for the last five months to keep the exchange rate of the yen from rising significantly, and thus hurting its competitive position.[21]

And in 1977, testifying before the same House subcommittee, Professor Aliber commented on Japanese and West German unwillingness to accept inflows of funds: "The currencies of Japan and to a lesser extent Germany are excessively depreciated relative to the dollar as a result of their unwillingness to borrow abroad to finance part of the increase in their oil import bill."[22]

The staff of the International Monetary Fund, in a July 1977 in-house paper surveying the world economy, commented obliquely on Japanese government policies to support the yen.

In Japan, the current account surplus in the first part
of 1977 was very large. . . . The recent appreciation
of the yen is to be welcomed . . . it is to be hoped
that the rate will not be affected significantly by administrative impediments to the inflow of capital.[23]

And a New York Times article in late 1977 commented that

this year the central banks have been very protective
of their home currencies. The Bank of Japan and
most of the European central banks have bought liter-
ally billions of dollars—selling yen, pounds, marks,
and Swiss francs—to try to keep their currencies from
rising so fast against the dollar.[24]

Despite awareness in most government policy-making circles,
and sometimes in public discussions, that it is the foreign-exchange
policies of Japan and West Germany that are behind their current-
account surpluses and the U.S. deficits, public discussion of the
Japanese and West German surpluses often gets tied up in extraneous
issues. One common line for U.S. commentators is to exalt the
discipline of the Japanese and West German workers or the aggres-
siveness of their overseas sales effort in contrast to the quarrel-
some, stubborn, and pampered U.S. labor force or the inferior U.S.
sales effort. Such a line is basically pro-U.S. business, for it often
leads to arguments to reduce the power of U.S. labor unions or to
increase government support for U.S. exports. It is also a misleading analysis: even if such gross national characterizations of greater
discipline and dedication to production were true, they would at most
explain the pace of economic growth and would not explain why Japan
and West Germany choose to export more than they import. High
productivity from a disciplined work force and from a dedicated
class of business entrepreneurs could be used entirely for higher
domestic consumption. High productivity does not necessarily lead
to a trade surplus.
    Another common mistaken position is to consider the trade
balance to be the result of various trade impediments such as tariffs
and quotas. In public discussions of the 1978 trade negotiations between Japan and the United States, the Japanese import quota on
orange juice seemed, for example, to be a major issue. It is most
likely that such issues are bargaining points that serve to mask the
primary concern over exchange rates that is expressed in the actual
private negotiations. Tariffs and quotas taken alone will influence
which goods a nation imports, but they will not determine the size
of the current-account surplus or deficit. With either a regime of
quotas and tariffs or a regime of absolutely free trade, a central

bank policy to purchase foreign exchange and control inflows of
funds will produce an undervalued exchange rate and a current-
account surplus. Thus, for the United States to complain about
quotas and tariffs or to impose its own quotas and tariffs may lead
to relief for certain export-oriented or import-competing industries,
but will do little or nothing for the overall deficits of the United
States or the surpluses of Japan and West Germany.

A third mistaken position is to consider the West German and
Japanese surpluses resulting from certain domestic constraints on
their economic policies; a fear of inflation is commonly cited. To
suppose that the fear of inflation is a valid reason not to adopt policies that would reduce a nation's current-account surplus is to accept an elaborate confusion which is no doubt deliberately encouraged
in some quarters. The argument that West Germany and Japan
should help shoulder the balancing deficits is often expressed in
terms of a recommendation that higher domestic growth would mean
more imports and a reduced current-account surplus. For U.S.
negotiators, recommendations for higher growth are no more than
a polite phrasing of the injunction to import more and export less,
but such recommendations are ultimately misleading, for they are
often turned around with the argument that the threat of inflation in
Japan and West Germany forces them to follow slow-growth policies
making it impossible for them to reduce their current-account surpluses. Whereas arguments over fast and slow growth are confus-
ing, a straightforward consideration of current-account surpluses,
exchange-rate manipulation, and inflation yields clear answers. It
is universally accepted that revaluation of a country's exchange rate
reduces domestic inflation through making imported goods cheaper
and also through shutting off some export sales, leaving more domestically produced goods for the domestic market. Revaluation,
which would result naturally if Japan and West Germany ceased to
buy dollars, would not only reduce the current-account surplus but
would also help to reduce inflationary pressures.

When the central banks of Japan and West Germany buy dollars
with yen and deutsche marks or lend yen and deutsche marks to foreign customers, such actions help to hold down the value of the yen
and deutsche mark and lead directly to current-account surpluses.
But in order to get the yen and marks used to buy dollars or to lend
to foreign customers, the central banks of Japan and West Germany
must either tax, borrow from domestic sources, or print the money.
Taxing reduces domestic purchasing power, borrowing both increases government debt and reduces the quantity of funds available
for domestic businesses to borrow, and printing money leads directly to inflation. Sluggish domestic demand, increased government
debt, and inflation are all symptoms of the economies of Japan and

West Germany in the late 1970s. To make the circle complete, some of the symptoms, such as rising government debt and inflation, are used as arguments against the expansionary programs that some people advocate to reduce the current-account surpluses. The symptoms are used to justify not doing anything about the surpluses, when everything that seems to be wrong—inflation, current-account surpluses, rising government debt, and so on—would be improved if the central banks of Japan and West Germany would simply permit the markets to revalue their currencies.

Japanese and West German Surpluses: Why?

This matter has been dealt with in part in Chapter 1; here we restate and make some further observations. Japanese and West German current-account surpluses are results of policies by their governments to purchase dollars, to discourage foreigners from investing in liquid short-term yen- and mark-denominated assets, and to give loans to foreign customers—in other words, to hold down the value of the yen and deutsche mark. Furthermore, such policies have domestic costs in terms of inflation, reduced domestic consumption and investment, and so forth. The next obvious question is why Japan and West Germany would want to make the effort for current-account surpluses.

Part of the answer lies in the desire for foreign investments. In 1976 Amaya, the Deputy Vice-Minister of Japan's Ministry of International Trade and Industry (MITI), explained Japan's need for foreign investment and indicated a role for the Japanese government in the drive to increase foreign investments.

> . . . it is necessary at present for Japan to invest large sums overseas. It is important to secure supplies. Resource-processing industries have to move overseas; also industries where costs can be reduced by moving overseas. It is difficult for private companies to do all this on their own account, therefore they depend on the Government.[25]

A senior economist from Japan Economic Research Center, Sueo Sekiguchi, wrote in early 1978 that "it is not expected that the current account surplus will suddenly be eliminated even if substantial measures are adopted to stimulate domestic demand. It is therefore forecasted that the balance of payments equilibrium will be achieved through increased outflows of long-term capital."[26] Japan, according to Sekiguchi, was looking forward to many years of current-account surpluses and increasing foreign investment.

The need for foreign investments by Japan and West Germany to protect access to markets and resources in other countries should be obvious in the light of recent disturbances in the international economic environment. Both Japan and West Germany realize that they are too dependent on U.S. firms in third countries and on U.S. diplomatic influence to maintain access to the foreign resources they need. A program of increased foreign investment is one thing that can be done by Japan and West Germany to improve the situation. By 1976 Japan had accumulated a total of only $10 billion in foreign direct investments, up from a minuscule $1.6 billion in 1970.[27] The United States in 1976 had a monstrous $137.2 billion in foreign direct investments, up from $75.5 billion in 1970.[28] West Germany in 1976 had $18.4 billion in foreign direct investment, and the rate of new foreign direct investment was nearly three times as high (in dollar terms) as it had been in 1970.[29] Given the relatively small total of Japanese and West German foreign direct investments to 1970, aggressive programs to increase foreign direct investments by Japan and West Germany were clearly called for in the 1970s.

As has been argued in Chapter 1, the surpluses of Japan and West Germany, by putting pressure on the U.S. trade and current-account balances, served as levers to get the United States to do something about its energy-import bills. The United States, faced with current-account deficits, could be forced into one or all of the following policies:

1. To reduce U.S. imports of oil: This would put downward pressure on the OPEC price of oil. It would also erode the rationale for U.S. influence in the Middle East. If the United States did not need and did not buy Middle East oil, then the oil-producing countries of the Middle East might be more willing to listen to arguments from Western European nations and Japan about the wisdom of bilateral trade ties that would bypass the Anglo-U.S. oil companies. The more exclusively Middle East and North African oil is directed to markets in Western Europe and Japan, the stronger will be direct ties between the two groups of countries.

2. To raise the price of energy in the United States: A U.S. policy of higher domestic oil prices, designed for conservation purposes to reduce U.S. dependence on oil imports, would help to bring U.S. energy costs up to those of its industrial competitors, thereby reducing the advantage the United States claimed for itself in 1973 by maintaining a controlled low price on domestically produced oil. Higher energy prices in the United States would reduce the advantage of U.S. producers in energy-intensive industries and would presumably affect the industrial location of, for example, new petrochemical investments.

3. <u>To put pressure on OPEC countries and the oil companies for a lower world price of oil</u>: Since 1973, the notion that world economic difficulties result from the high price of OPEC oil has been repeatedly used as an argument against higher world oil prices whenever the OPEC nations meet to discuss future price increases. But high oil prices would not have been a serious problem without high current-account surpluses in Japan and West Germany. Thus, by running large current-account surpluses, Japan and West Germany kept alive the argument that further OPEC oil price increases would be destabilizing.

The United States, whose monstrous and painful deficits in 1977 and 1978 demonstrate its commitment to the present system of multilateral trade and currency exchange, is the natural target of Japanese and West German threats: U.S. trade is most hurt by competition from Japan and West Germany, the United States is most committed to the current multilateral trade and exchange system, and the United States of all powers has the most influence over oil companies and oil countries. If U.S. pressure through the oil companies and the oil countries were able to prevent further price increases, then the U.S. current-account balance would be improved directly through a lower oil-import bill and indirectly through a decreased need to accept the balancing deficits that others do not want.

If pressures to reduce the price of oil are successful, or if the oil cartel is weakened through a reduction in U.S. oil imports, then the position of the United States in world oil would be severely damaged. The oil countries know what their oil is worth, and if the United States is unable to protect a stable system of trade that maintains prices and income flows, it would be very difficult to prevent an eventual shift in the loyalties of OPEC nations to Western European countries and to Japan, countries that in any case buy most of OPEC's oil and are ready and willing to cut in whenever the United States falters.

Surpluses by Japan and West Germany serve as well to increase the already formidable monetary reserves of the Japanese and West German central banks, a development which increases the importance of Japan and West Germany in international economic affairs. In 1977, West Germany held $40 billion worth of international reserves, Japan held $23 billion, and the United States had $19 billion. (A government's international reserves include its holdings of gold, foreign exchange, and a few other items; in these figures, holdings of gold are valued at the official price, far below its market value.) Large holdings of international reserves in West Germany and Japan in the late 1970s increase the influence of those two countries whenever there is a foreign-exchange crisis in another nation or whenever reforms for the international financial system are under discussion.

The value to a country of large holdings of international reserves—especially when the international economic system is in flux—can be seen in the experience of the United States after World War II. An important component of U.S. international economic power after the war was its massive stock of gold, which had been built up during the depression and World War II. In 1948, the U.S. government owned $24 billion worth of gold, an amount equivalent to three-quarters of all the gold held by all governments in the noncommunist world. With its large stock of gold, along with its general economic strength, the United States was able to dictate the design of post-World War II international financial agreements and in particular to establish control over the design and operation of the International Monetary Fund. Whenever new regional or international monetary agreements are negotiated in the 1980s, Japanese and West German international reserves will be important weapons with which to promote Japanese and West German interests.

Continued central bank intervention in foreign-exchange markets in order to insure current-account surpluses for Japan and West Germany is putting the United States in a difficult situation. In 1971, in an analogous situation (at that time Japan and West Germany were buying dollars to maintain fixed exchange rates that the United States felt were too low), the United States broke up the system of fixed exchange rates in order to permit the dollar to be devalued and to force the yen and deutsche mark to be revalued. In the late 1970s, the currencies are floating, but massive purchases of dollars by central banks around the world have again resulted in an overvalued dollar and even larger trade deficits. To defend itself against such behavior by foreign central banks, the United States may decide to institute exchange controls, preventing foreign central banks from investing their purchased dollars in U.S. government bonds and other dollar-denominated assets. Controls would discourage foreign central banks from buying dollars (since they could no longer be invested to earn interest) and would thereby free the value of the dollar from control by foreign central banks, making it possible for the United States to once again run trade and current-account surpluses.

If and when the United States does limit use of the dollar as a reserve currency, it will signify a major retrenchment in the design of what has been the postwar U.S. empire. It would be the turning point from an open multilateral system with the United States at the center to a system of several currency and trade blocs, each led by a key industrial nation.

A future of trade and currency blocs (the yen bloc, the deutsche mark bloc, the dollar bloc, and so forth) is the logical and inevitable outcome of continued policies by West Germany and Japan to force the United States into deficits. Such a development would present problems particularly for the United States, which has by far the largest share of foreign investment; U.S. firms in countries that join some bloc other than the dollar bloc would be hostages in inter-bloc negotiations and competition. Both Japan and West Germany, whose shares of world exports of manufactures are about equal to that of the United States, would be able to develop a substantial group of client countries and would probably find themselves with a more secure and sheltered economic environment than they have experienced in the 1970s. The increases in the price of oil during the 1970s surely pushed Japan and West Germany to follow down the path of self-reliance in international economics. Anticipating the eventual establishment of a yen bloc and a deutsche mark bloc, the surpluses of Japan and West Germany serve to permit the anticipatory build-up of international reserves and foreign investment and influence in selected countries.

For its part, the United States is trying to maintain the multilateral system based on the dollar as long as possible. When currency and trade blocs are formed, the United States will find restricted access to markets and resources in other blocs. U.S. foreign investments within other blocs will face the problem of a loss of U.S. government influence in the host country. Profits will be eroded by policies of host-country governments designed to favor companies from West Germany (if it is a deutsche mark bloc country) or Japan (if a yen bloc country).

A particular problem is posed by oil. The United States has attempted to prevent what it calls "bilateral" trade between oil-producing and oil-importing countries. Package deals of oil for weapons or factories, for example, between an oil producer and an oil importer reduce the role of U.S. oil companies and ultimately threaten U.S. influence over world oil. Such bilateral deals may be seen as foundation stones for developing deutsche mark and yen blocs, for oil is one of the most crucial and most expensive items in foreign trade. The less Japan and West Germany have to pay for oil in dollars or rely on U.S. good will to maintain a flow of oil, the weaker are the centripetal forces holding together the dollar bloc of today, otherwise known as the multilateral system of world trade and currency exchange.

The current-account surpluses of Japan and West Germany can be explained as serving a number of interests for West Germany and Japan. In all respects, U.S. interests are hurt in direct proportion to the benefits gained by West Germany and Japan. The pressure of continued current-account surpluses has been used in the late 1970s as a lever for lower world oil prices. In a long-term perspective, it is U.S. preeminence in international economic affairs and especially in oil that is the target of attack. Sooner or later, continued large current-account surpluses in Japan and West Germany will force the United States to retrench, to set more modest geographical limits on the dollar bloc, and to make more room in the world for Japan and West Germany.

THE ECONOMIC IMPACT OF HIGH OIL PRICES: REALITY AND RHETORIC

One consistent theme in international economic negotiations between the United States, Japan, and West Germany since 1973 has been the heavy burden of high oil prices on the economies of the oil-importing nations. On closer examination, nobody has been hurt very badly by high oil prices. Still, all the moaning serves a purpose: nations since 1973 have used high oil prices as excuses or arguments for uncooperative or aggressive behavior. The breakdown of cooperation between the big three, which was already clear in Nixon's 1971 unilateral abrogation of the Bretton Woods system, has since 1973 been masked by continual reference to high oil prices as the excuse for chauvinistic economic policies.

The economic impact of high oil prices may be measured very simply in the cost of oil imports for the various countries (Table 4.4). Japan, with its industrialized economy and its heavy dependence on imported oil, was the most severely affected nation in the world in terms of GNP paid out for higher-priced oil. In 1974 the cost of oil to Japan came to 4.66 percent of GNP, up from 1.50 percent in 1972. For Germany, oil-import bills came to 3.26 percent of GNP in 1974, up from 1.29 percent in 1972. By comparison with 1972, post-1973 experience shows an increase in import costs of as much as 2 to 3 percent of GNP for the most seriously affected industrial countries. As has been noted already, the United States was hurt less severely by the oil price increase than were the nations of Western Europe and Japan. The increase in the oil-import bill of the United States reflects not only higher prices but also higher volumes of oil.

Although the oil tax may seem large in terms of aggregate figures and in terms of a percent of GNP, there is another way to look at the matter. Sidney Alexander has pointed out that "Only six months' growth of output, at the rates of the 1960s, would be required for the developed countries to absorb the extra costs of oil imports; and less than three months for the less developed countries."[30] Since the most seriously affected country, Japan, was on such a high growth trajectory, only about four months' normal growth would have made up for its oil tax. That this growth was not normal is another matter; hypothetically, the increased cost of oil in world markets would not have had to set any nation back in its pursuit of affluence more than a matter of months.

TABLE 4.4

Oil Import Bills as a Percentage of GNP

	United States	West Germany	Japan
1970	0.281	1.26	—*
1971	0.312	1.48	1.60
1972	0.367	1.29	1.50
1973	0.587	1.63	1.64
1974	1.72	3.26	4.66
1975	1.64	2.81	4.28
1976	1.85	3.13	4.20
1977	2.18	2.88	3.77
1978	1.83	2.52	2.90

*Not available.

Source: International Monetary Fund, International Financial Statistics 30, 11 (Washington, D.C.: IMF, November 1977), pp. 148-51, 204-7, 368-71; and 32, 5 (May 1979), pp. 154-57, 212-15, 388-91.

The impact of higher oil prices on the distribution of current-account surpluses and deficits is a more serious problem. Still, high oil prices would not have been seriously destabilizing if the big three had been able to cooperate. U.S. efforts to maintain the multilateral trade and payments system based on the dollar have since 1973 been discussed largely in terms of the "problem of adjustment" to OPEC surpluses, when the true problem is noncooperation among the big three. The threat of world depression in conjunction with a possible breakdown of the dollar bloc is less and less credible to Japan and Western Europe; with establishment of yen and deutsche mark blocs, businesses in West Germany and Japan would likely find acceptable and stable long-term prospects. Still, the United States continues to defend its vast dollar bloc under the banner of saving the multilateral trade and payments system from the destabilizing consequences of higher world oil prices.

OIL POWER VERSUS CURRENT-
ACCOUNT SURPLUSES

In 1974 Helmut Schmidt saw a "struggle for the world product."
In 1972, C. Fred Bergsten, formerly an advisor to the National
Security Council, had already speculated on the future course of
economic disagreements among the industrialized nations.

> The United States may . . . be tempted to employ the
> principle of comparative bargaining advantage by trying
> to use its security leverage to pursue its economic ob-
> jectives; the United States might even seek to maintain
> (or expand) its politico-military role in the world for
> this purpose.
> In response, Europe and Japan might refuse to
> play either because they thought that the United States
> was bluffing, given its own security interests, or be-
> cause of their own perceptions of the relative impor-
> tance of their economic targets vis-a-vis the real
> risks to their security. Or they might even try to
> use their economic leverage to pursue political ob-
> jectives, as de Gaulle did.[31]

In supporting higher oil prices the United States did use its
"politico-military" advantage to support its economic interests
against Japan and West Germany. In response, West Germany and
Japan have been using "economic leverage to pursue political ob-
jectives," in this case, to get the United States to do something
about oil.

NOTES

1. Helmut Schmidt, "The Struggle for the World Product,"
in The World Economic Crisis, ed. William Bundy (New York:
Norton, 1975), p. 110.
2. Discrepancies may arise because some goods are in
transit, because nations may use different accounting practices,
and because of errors and omissions.
3. Brookings Institution, "The World Economy in Transition"
(Tripartite Report) (Washington, D.C., 1975), p. 6.
4. Citibank, Economics Department, "OPEC Spends Its Way
to Growth," Economic Week (October 16, 1978).
5. "Text of the Final Communique" (Washington Energy Conference), quoted in Stockholm International Peace Research Institute,
Oil and Security (New York: Humanities Press, 1974), p. 125.

6. Brookings Institution, "Cooperative Approaches to World Energy Problems" (Tripartite Report) (Washington, D.C., 1974), p. 18.

7. Schmidt, p. 115.

8. Sidney Alexander, "Background Paper," Paying for Energy, Report of the Twentieth Century Fund Task Force on the International Oil Crisis (New York: McGraw-Hill, 1975), p. 84.

9. Ibid., p. 85.

10. There are some small sources of oil on the world market aside from OPEC exports. The most important has been the Soviet Union, with oil exports equivalent to 3-5 percent of OPEC oil exports through this period.

11. Alexander, p. 82. The OECD countries (mentioned in the quote) are listed in Table 4.2.

12. International Monetary Fund, "World Economic Outlook— A General Survey" (Washington, D.C.: IMF, 1977), pp. 16, 17.

13. Ibid.

14. Testimony of Paul Watson, in U.S. Congress, Senate, Committee on Banking, Housing and Urban Affairs, Subcommittee on International Finance, International Debt, 95th Cong., 1st sess., August 30, 1977, p. 197.

15. U.S. Congress, Senate Committee on Foreign Relations, Subcommittee on Foreign Economic Policy, The Witteveen Facility and the OPEC Financial Surpluses, 95th Cong., 1st sess., October 10, 1977, pp. 129-30.

16. Testimony of Robert Z. Aliber, in U.S. Congress, House, Committee on Banking, Finance and Urban Affairs, Subcommittee on International Trade, Investment and Monetary Policy, U.S. Participation in the Supplementary Financing Facility of the International Monetary Fund, 95th Cong., 1st sess., September 20, 1977, p. 173.

17. Testimony of C. Fred Bergsten, in U.S. Congress, House, Committee on Banking, Currency and Housing, Subcommittee on International Trade, Investment and Monetary Policy, To Provide for Amendment of the Bretton Woods Agreements Act, 94th Cong., 2d sess., June 3, 1976, p. 99.

18. Bundesbank, Monthly Report of the Deutsche Bundesbank, 29, 7 (July 1977), p. 16.

19. For Japan, for example, to loan yen that must be repaid in a few years means that the nonresident buying Japanese goods does not have to buy yen today but can wait and buy when the loan is due. This lowers demand for yen on foreign exchange markets and helps to reduce today's yen value. Since new loans are constantly being made, and since the volume of loans increases year by year, the value of the yen is consistently depressed by delaying the day

when nonresident customers have to go to foreign exchange markets to buy yen.

20. U.S. Congress, House, Committee on Banking, Currency and Housing, Subcommittee on International Trade, Investment and Monetary Policy, Oversight Hearings on the Export-Import Bank, 94th Cong., 2d sess., August 1976, pp. 66, 53, 71.

21. Bergsten (testimony), p. 98.

22. Aliber (testimony), p. 180.

23. IMF, p. 23.

24. Geoffrey Bell, "Who Cares If the Dollar Sinks?" New York Times, December 25, 1977, Sec. 3, p. 1.

25. Robin Pringle, "Japanese Puzzles," The Banker 126, 607 (September 1976): 1051.

26. Sueo Sekiguchi, "Japan on the Threshold of Becoming a Capital Exporter," Wall Street Journal, March 23, 1978.

27. Ibid.

28. U.S. Department of Commerce, Statistical Abstract of the United States 1978 (Washington, D.C.: Government Printing Office, 1978), p. 864.

29. Bundesbank, "Reversal in the Balance of Direct Investments," Monthly Report of the Deutsche Bundesbank, 30, 10 (October 1978), p. 34; Bundesbank, "The Level of Direct Investment at the End of 1976," Deutsche Bundesbank, 31, 4 (April 1979), p. 27.

30. Alexander, pp. 72-73.

31. C. Fred Bergsten, "The Future of the International Economic Order: An Agenda for Research," in The Future of the International Economic Order, ed. C. Fred Bergsten (Lexington, Mass.: Lexington, 1973), p. 31.

5

INTERNATIONAL ECONOMICS AFTER 1973: DEBTORS AND CREDITORS

Since the 1973 oil-price increases boosted the revenues of OPEC nations, there has been a steady flow of OPEC money into U.S. bank deposits and U.S. government debt. Capital markets in the U.S. have in turn made loans to the deficit nations to help them pay their current foreign bills. In the process, the United States has become, in the words of Senator Jacob Javits, the "obligated middleman" in international finance.[1] Although Senator Javits and many others have been critical of the situation, a more favorable interpretation is possible: U.S. institutions gain power and profits from their use of borrowed OPEC funds.

As financial "middleman" the United States has one major problem: Japan and West Germany have added their current-account surpluses on top of the OPEC surpluses, increasing the size of the balancing deficits necessary for other nations. With the uncooperative behavior of Japan and West Germany, it has been a difficult matter to spread the deficits around. For some nations (for example, England and Italy) large deficits are associated with unemployment. For others (like Brazil and Mexico) large deficits increase already troublesome levels of international debt. Many observers have become critical of further U.S. bank loans to major debtors among the less developed countries. Despite these problems, by 1977 and 1978 the distribution of current-account deficits among nations (with the United States taking a large deficit) was such that deficits, debt burdens, and rates of lending seemed to be sustainable for the foreseeable future. The reduction of OPEC surpluses to $11 billion in 1978 provided further relief for the deficit nations. However, in the context of continued conflict between Japan, West Germany, and the United States, creditors and debtors remained worried about the future.

An essential feature of international investment and international debt is that political issues are always involved. Accordingly, this chapter begins with a discussion of some of the political aspects

of international lending. Later sections deal with several of the
many components of the present system of international finance:
nations that save, nations that borrow, nations that play the role of
financial intermediary, the private banks, and the International
Monetary Fund.

POLITICAL ASPECTS OF INTERNATIONAL LENDING

Within the context of an ordered, lawful society, one person in
debt to another can be forced to pay by law. If the debtor will not
willingly honor a contract, the creditor can simply bring the matter
to court. If the debtor has the money to pay, the debt is paid; if the
debtor does not have sufficient funds, the creditor must accept a
loss, and that is the end of the creditor's claims on the debtor—even
if the former debtor later comes into wealth.

In the context of international relations, there are several
crucial differences in the creditor-debtor relationship. First, the
debtor cannot be forced by law to pay; the conduct of international
affairs among nations is still decided at least potentially through
threats on the prosperity and well-being of citizens of one country
by citizens of another. In practice, debtors who do not meet con-
tractual terms as specified by creditor nations are usually dealt
with, at least initially, through economic sanctions: the creditor
nations attempt to interrupt the normal flow of international trade
for the debtor nation. Often such economic sanctions are part of a
wider program to weaken the ability of the current leaders of the
debtor government to hold power and to bring the return of a "responsible" government, through a coup if necessary. What happened
to Chile in 1973 is at least in part an example of the process of
creditor enforcement.

A second difference that distinguishes international from
domestic debt is that there is no equivalent to bankruptcy in international relations whereby a nation may shed its international debt.
Creditors retain their international claims on debtor nations even
though the government of the debtor nation is unable to pay, repu-
diates the debt outright, or otherwise tries to alter the contract. If
the government of the debtor nation asks for mercy and promises to
cooperate so as to protect its future credit rating, the debts are
usually rescheduled or, in other words, they are postponed (with
interest, of course) so that the debtor government is faced with a
heavier future repayment bill. International debts are rarely for-
gotten; claims on prerevolutionary China, for example, were held
for years against the possibility that at some future time the Chinese
government would be interested in clearing past accounts to smooth
future trade relations.

Since debt relations between various nations are not automatically enforced by some supranational court, and since debts are intermittently challenged by debtor nations unwilling or unable to pay, a nation would be foolish to loan money to any nation over which it had no influence. But since the exercise of foreign influence to insure repayment can easily damage good relations between creditor and debtor nations, creditor nations often try to restrain the growth of international debt. Thus, relations of international debt always have a political, as well as an economic, dimension. This political dimension affects, for example, the behavior of the OPEC nations as investors and largely determines the source of funds for deficit and debtor states.

NATIONS THAT SAVE

The price increases of 1973 and later pushed the foreign-exchange earnings of several of the OPEC nations beyond any reasonable increase in import expenditures; the most important chronic surplus countries in OPEC have been Saudi Arabia, Iran, Kuwait, and the United Arab Emirates. Over the same period, vigorous export expansion by several European countries and Japan raised their foreign exchange earnings beyond the increase in their oil-import bills. Governments, corporations, and residents of the two groups of surplus countries have come to hold large amounts of surplus foreign-exchange earnings in the form of bank deposits, the bonds of foreign governments, and other investments in foreign countries.

Among the 13 OPEC states, only four stand out for their consistently large surpluses. Of the cumulative total of about $180 billion in OPEC surplus earnings from 1974 through 1977, Saudi Arabia alone has accounted for $64 billion (35 percent), Iran and Kuwait have accounted for $26 billion (14 percent) and $25 billion (14 percent) respectively, and the United Arab Emirates has taken $19 billion (10.5 percent). Although Iraq and Libya could become large-surplus countries given the size and nature of their oil reserves, their current-account surpluses through 1977 have not yet come close to those of the other four. Of the other seven OPEC nations, Qatar, with about 2 percent of OPEC oil exports, has run consistent current-account surpluses of about $1 billion. Gabon and Ecuador each have less than 1 percent of OPEC sales and have either had small current-account surpluses or deficits since 1973. Indonesia, Algeria, Nigeria, and Venezuela all ran current-account deficits in 1977. Thus, in talking about OPEC surpluses and how they are invested, we need only pay attention to four OPEC states:

Saudi Arabia, Iran, Kuwait, and the United Arab Emirates. (The current-account positions of OPEC nations for 1971 to 1977 are shown in Table 5.1.)

Most of OPEC's surplus foreign earnings are invested abroad by the separate governments rather than by individuals or businesses. The Saudi Arabian Monetary Authority, for example, increased its foreign assets by $34 billion from the end of 1973 to the end of 1975, while Saudi Arabian current-account surpluses for that period totaled $37 billion. [2]

Governments of the four OPEC countries with the largest surpluses have directed most of their foreign investments to the United States and Great Britain. From the OPEC point of view, this is the safest investment possible, for the OPEC states have hostage within their borders the assets of U.S. and British oil companies; any threat by the United States or Great Britain to expropriate OPEC investments could always be countered by moves against the oil companies. A 1977 staff report to the Senate Subcommittee on Foreign Economic Policy explained the preferences of the OPEC investors as follows:

> There are both political and financial reasons why [the
> United States and Great Britain] are favored over other
> industrial countries. In the first place they have close
> political and military ties with the three oil producers
> which account for most of the surpluses: Saudi Arabia,
> Kuwait and the UAE. The United States and Britain
> are also the home base of the seven major oil com-
> panies . . . which are the main business partners of
> the oil producing governments. [3]

Iran should have been listed in the quote, both for its large surpluses (at least through 1977) and close military ties with the United States but, nevertheless, the point is well made: the United States and Great Britain have together received the lion's share of foreign investments by the oil-exporting nations. After an early 1976 study tour to the Middle East, Senator Adlai Stevenson reported with approval that he was confident of a "continued flow of Saudi capital and oil to meet U.S. needs." [4] According to the report cited above, "Both the United States and the United Kingdom have sought actively to attract OPEC funds." [5]

Aside from favoring the United States and to a lesser extent Great Britain in their investment plans, the OPEC saving states have favored secure fixed-interest investments such as U.S. government debt and bank deposits in major U.S. and European banks. Purchases of stock in Pan Am, Krupp, or some other major

TABLE 5.1

Current-Account Balances of OPEC Nations and of Other Key Surplus States
($ millions)

	1971	1972	1973	1974	1975	1976	1977	1974-77
OPEC states								
Algeria	43	-124	-443	160	-1,661	-883	-2,322	-4,706
Ecuador	-156	-77	7	37.6	-220	-6.3	-312	-501
Gabon	18	-4	-36	209.6	58	27.8	43	338
Indonesia	-372	-334	-476	598	-1,109	-907	-51	-1,469
Iran	-118	-358	154	12,267	4,207	4,714	5,081	26,269
Iraq	193	546	801	2,619	2,705	1,800*	n.a.	n.a.
Kuwait	n.a.	n.a.	n.a.	6,300*	5,891	6,971	5,456	24,600
Libya	283	238	66	1,832	-68	2,435	2,905	7,140
Nigeria	-406	-342	-8	4,897	42	-342	-897	3,700
Qatar	n.a.	n.a.	n.a.	1,100*	1,000*	1,000*	n.a.	n.a.
Saudi Arabia	91	1,473	2,203	23,007	13,978	13,978	12,793	63,709
United Arab Emirates	n.a.	n.a.	n.a.	4,100*	4,100*	5,500*	n.a.	n.a.
Venezuela	86	-39	899	5,862	2,394	967	-2,053	7,170
Total for surplus states only	n.a.	n.a.	n.a.	63,000	34,800	37,400	n.a.	n.a.
Other states								
Japan	5,797	6,624	-136	-4,693	-682	3,680	10,911	9,216
West Germany	875	747	4,371	9,804	4,059	3,902	3,799	21,569
Switzerland	80	220	280	171	2,587	3,518	3,782	10,058
Netherlands	-182	1,302	2,214	1,960	2,001	2,691	245	6,897

n.a.: not available.

*Data from "The Big Spenders: Where the Oil Money has Gone," The Banker (March 1977), p. 91.

Source: International Monetary Fund, International Financial Statistics, 31, 12 (Washington, D.C.: IMF, December 1978).

corporation by OPEC investors makes news, but such acquisitions comprise only a small part of total OPEC investments. Nor do OPEC countries allocate a significant portion of their surpluses for direct loans to the governments of deficit Third World countries, except for a few Islamic states. That the OPEC governments avoid direct investments in major corporations or direct loans to Third World countries is reasonable: such investments are too easily identifiable and thereby expose the wealth of the investor to disgruntled jealousy and perhaps even confiscation (or loan default). In a 1974 article in <u>Foreign Affairs</u>, Gerald Pollack, a senior economic advisor for Exxon, explained that, as investors, OPEC governments want "anonymity—a valuable feature to governments anxious to avoid creating 'hostages' abroad."[6]

Although the foreign assets of several of the OPEC countries are so large that an abrupt shift out of, for example, U.S. bank deposits into West German stocks would be destabilizing to the banks and to the value of the dollar, such an action would make no sense; nor do fears of such an action receive any support from the investment behavior of the key surplus states. The power of any OPEC government is based on oil. Any attempt to use foreign investment for political or diplomatic ends could be countered by simple refusal to let the OPEC state cash in its investments or move its funds out of banks or government debt. To defend its investments in such a confrontation, the OPEC government would have to threaten confiscation of oil-company assets or it could threaten to withhold oil. Since the use of financial power would, in any case, have to be backed up by oil power, and since exercise of oil power has so far been a matter of cooperation between OPEC nations, oil companies, and home countries, the desire and ability of any OPEC nation to do anything unsettling with its foreign investments is hardly likely. When and if any OPEC government decides to flex its muscle in international affairs, it will most likely be through oil rather than anything that would draw attention to its highly vulnerable foreign investments. Finally, the key saving states of OPEC have been cooperating with the United States in their investment plans: they have been partners, not adversaries. Until the basic alliance between the United States and the oil-exporting countries over the control of oil breaks down, the basis for financial cooperation is secure.[7]

The four key surplus states among the OPEC nations are not, however, the four major surplus states in the world. Over the four years from 1974 to 1977, the cumulative current-account surpluses of West Germany ($22 billion) placed it fourth among surplus states in the world after Saudi Arabia, Iran, and Kuwait, but ahead of the United Arab Emirates. In 1978, Japan had the largest yearly current-account surplus, with Saudi Arabia in second place.

As discussed in Chapter 4, Japan and West Germany (and Switzerland as well) have bought dollars in foreign-exchange markets to insure for themselves a current-account surplus; they have invested the purchased dollars in U.S. government deblt. The governments of both OPEC and non-OPEC surplus countries thus find themselves lending money to the United States. The United States, however, is not equally satisfied with such similar behavior by the two groups of surplus countries. Saudi Arabia, for example, is supporting U.S. economic influence in the world by pricing its oil in dollars, keeping its assets in dollars, and putting its money in U.S. banks. West Germany and Japan, on the other hand, buy and hold dollars in order to run a current-account surplus at the expense of the United States. Nevertheless, both OPEC and non-OPEC investments in the United States increase U.S. financial power, giving it more funds to relend or to reinvest elsewhere in the world.

Although both Japan and West Germany do invest in U.S. government debt, they are much more than passive investors in their international economic relations with the rest of the world. Both nations are able to attract foreign funds (such as foreign direct investment by U.S. multinationals or OPEC bank deposits in their large commercial banks). Both nations are anxious to establish their corporations and banks in the international economy. Unlike the OPEC investors, which seek anonymity and which must cooperate with patron states among the developed countries in order to insure the security of their foreign investments, Japan and West Germany are able to defend their investments with a variety of economic and diplomatic weapons. Despite the billions in foreign exchange reserves held by their governments, much of the foreign assets acquired by Japan and West Germany are managed by corporations and banks.

NATIONS THAT BORROW

In general, nations with current-account deficits borrow from foreign sources in order to pay the excess of foreign expenses over foreign receipts. Since 1973 the increase in deficits by non-OPEC, non-big-three nations has resulted in a vast increase in the volume of their international borrowing. Who has borrowed, from whom they have borrowed, and the seriousness of the accumulating debt burdens have been matters of continuing concern since 1973.

Of the 11 nations with the largest cumulative current-account deficits from 1974 through 1977 (Table 5.2), only two (Brazil and Norway) have had average deficits larger than 5 percent of GNP over those four years. All but four (Brazil, Mexico, Norway, and Australia) had cumulative current-account surpluses in the four preceding

TABLE 5.2

Countries with the Largest Cumulative
Current-Account Deficits, 1974-77

	Current-Account Balance 1970-73		Current-Account Balance 1974-77	
	Cumulative Total ($ millions)	As % of GNP Average of Yearly Values	Cumulative Total ($ millions)	As % of GNP Average of Yearly Values
Brazil	-6,046	-2.5	-25,969	-5.1
France	433	0.1	-15,294	-1.2
United Kingdom	2,358	0.6	-14,031	-1.7
Canada	1,233	0.4	-13,954	-2.0
Norway	-1,190	-2.2	-12,402	-10.0
Spain	1,433	1.1	-12,213	-3.1
Mexico	-4,242	-1.6	-12,106	-4.7
Italy	2,997	0.8	-9,165	-1.4
Sweden	1,433	0.7	-8,322	-3.0
Turkey	693	0.8	-7,761	-4.7
Australia	-648	-0.7	-7,174	-2.1
Israel	-1,399	-5.5	-5,524	-11.6
South Africa	-2,870	-3.9	-5,192	-3.8
Denmark	-1,494	-2.0	-5,028	-3.4
Finland	-1,087	-2.1	-4,714	-4.6
Algeria	-650	-2.3	-4,706	-7.3
Greece	-2,365	-4.4	-4,605	-5.2
Peru	-124	-0.1	-4,378	-8.6
Portugal	—*	—*	-4,307	-7.1
South Korea	-2,148	-5.8	-4,215	-5.9
New Zealand	544	1.5	-3,938	-7.4
Yugoslavia	193	0.6	-3,670	-3.0
Pakistan	-1,461	-4.1	-3,471	-7.6
Egypt	-454	-1.9	-3,345	-6.0
Philippines	436	1.0	-3,064	-4.3
Austria	-625	-0.6	-3,002	-3.1

*Not available.
Source: International Monetary Fund, International Financial Statistics, 30, 11 (Washington, D.C.: IMF, November 1977), and 31, 12 (December 1978).

years, 1970 through 1973. And for only three (Brazil, Mexico, and Turkey) have their volumes of international debt been a problem in the past. Thus, for most of the nations with large current-account deficits in the years since 1973, the buildup of foreign debt related to large continuing deficits has not been a problem.

Although debt has not been a problem for many of the largest deficit nations, this does not mean that the deficits in themselves have not been a problem. For Italy and Great Britain, for example, current-account deficits in 1974 of 5.1 and 4.3 percent of GNP, respectively, created tremendous internal political pressures, bringing in new economic policies that led to current-account surpluses for both nations by 1977. For these nations, the problem of current-account deficits was not that borrowing could not be arranged, but rather that a large excess of imports over exports interfered with domestic production; industrialists and union members saw current-account deficits hurting profits, wages, and employment.

From the point of view of those interested in maintaining international economic stability and free trade, the two biggest matters of concern related to the deficits of such nations as Italy, Great Britain, Canada, France, Sweden, Australia, and other nations with strong export potential and low debt burdens has been that the deficits should continue and that the deficit nations should not use quotas, tariffs, or other infringements on free trade in an effort to get rid of the deficits. If the strong nations do not run balancing deficits, who will? And if a major trading nation opts out of the system of free trade, the danger is that trade restrictions could multiply internationally, leading to international recession in the short run and to more and more government control over business in the long run. Free trade and free enterprise would be in jeopardy. Consequently, the sum of international pressures on Italy, Great Britain, Canada, France, and other strong nations has been that their deficits continue. The deficits of the United States in 1977 and 1978 must be seen in the same light: such deficits make it possible for other nations that cannot bear deficits so easily to have smaller ones. Pressure for the strong nations to limit or to eliminate current-account deficits has come in most cases from domestic political groups, not from foreign creditors or other interested foreign parties.

Deficit nations without debt problems and with strong economies (including many of the nations listed in Table 5.2) are able to borrow from private, foreign capital markets without having to ask for loans from governments or international institutions. The government of such a debtor country may, for example, encourage corporations to borrow abroad by maintaining high domestic interest rates and tight credit. With such an inhospitable domestic credit market, resident corporations may find it cheaper to sell bonds in foreign markets or to go to nonresident banks for a loan in some foreign currency; the foreign exchange raised in such a manner may be exchanged for domestic currencies. Alternatively, the government of a deficit nation may borrow foreign exchange on its own in foreign or international bond markets or from banks.

Among the developed nations, even very large deficits may never lead to a need for government borrowing from other governments or from multilateral institutions. The decisions by the Italian and British governments to seek loans from the International Monetary Fund in 1974 and 1976, respectively, were motivated in part by the desire of governing groups to shift responsibility for unpopular new economic policies to the IMF (which makes its loans conditional on policy changes by the borrowing government) and to dramatize the seriousness of the economic situation so as to make people more willing to accept any difficulties that might be experienced.

International debt—as distinct from deficits—has in general been a problem for the less developed countries rather than the developed countries. The international debt of less developed countries can be of many types. Governments may borrow from other governments, multilateral institutions, foreign banks, or foreign bond markets. Corporations and banks resident in the less developed country may borrow from foreign banks or foreign bond markets. Most of the time, however, only borrowing by the government of the less developed country—whether from official or private sources—is considered in discussions of its international debt burdens. Since external government debt is usually considered separately from the foreign debts of the private sector for any nation with repayment difficulties, it is generally appropriate to consider only governments' external debts in discussions of debt burdens.

Since 1973, the non-oil less developed countries have been intensively examined for debt difficulties related to large new deficits. Although the period 1974-75 brought very large deficits, by 1976 and 1977 aggregate current-account deficits for these countries had been brought into line with pre-1973 experience. Moreover, inflation had reduced the burden of previous deficits. According to testimony by Paul Watson to the Senate Subcommittee on International Finance, "The total present value of debt service payments due over the period of 1973 to 1982 on public debt outstanding at the end of 1972 was reduced by nearly 40 percent by inflation during 1973-1976 alone."[8]

Table 5.3 lists the less developed countries with the largest volume of external public debt in 1975 along with one key measure of the burden of external public debt: the value of yearly debt-service

TABLE 5.3

Developing Countries[a] with External Public Debts[b]
over $1.3 Billion
(1975, disbursed only)

	External Public Debt ($ billions)	Payments of Interest and Principle as a Percentage of Exports of Goods and Nonfactor Services			
		1970–73 (average)	1974	1975	1976
India	12.3	21.9	17.2	13.4	12.0
Brazil	11.6	14.6	12.0	14.6	14.8
Mexico	11.6	23.0	18.7	25.0	32.3
Indonesia	8.1	6.7	3.9	8.1	11.2
South Korea	5.5	17.4	9.6	10.1	8.9
Pakistan	5.5	20.7	15.4	18.4	18.2
Algeria	4.5	8.4	13.5[c]	8.8	14.1
Egypt	4.2	32.1	20.8	21.5	17.6
Iran	3.8	14.8	6.9	4.1	4.3
Chile	3.7	15.2	11.5	28.6	32.9
Spain	3.4	3.8	2.4	2.6	3.6
Turkey	3.1	11.6	6.4	7.4	7.1
Argentina	2.9	20.0	16.6	21.4	18.3
Peru	2.7	20.7	23.9[c]	23.4	21.6
Greece	2.6	8.7	8.7	10.5	11.2
Colombia	2.4	12.8	15.8	11.1	9.4
Yugoslavia	2.3	6.0	5.5	5.7	5.5
Morocco	1.7	8.8	5.3	6.8	8.2
Zaire	1.7	6.4	12.9	15.8	11.7
Taiwan	1.6	4.1	2.6	3.9	3.5
Bangladesh	1.6	2.2[d]	6.0	17.9	13.4
Philippines	1.4	8.3	3.3	7.3	6.6
Malaysia	1.3	2.7	2.6	3.5	4.3

[a]This list of developing countries includes the more developed Mediterranean countries as well as the oil exporters along with the non-oil less developed countries.

[b]External public debt includes all external debt owed or insured by the government; debts with an original maturity of less than one year are not counted.

[c]These figures include some prepayments and are thus biased upward.

[d]1973 value only.

Source: World Bank, World Debt Tables, vol. 1 (Washington, D.C.: World Bank, 1978), Tables 1A and 12A.

payments (interest plus repayment of principle) as a percent of exports. Several more developed Mediterranean countries (Spain, Greece, Turkey, and Yugoslavia) are listed as well. For many of the largest debtors, the burden of external debt had eased between 1970-73 and 1975. This is significant because 1974 and 1975 were years of record borrowing by non-oil less developed countries. inflation and expanding exports had helped to hold down the burden of interest and repayment obligations on external public debts as a percentage of export sales.

For several of the largest debtors (India, Pakistan, Bangladesh, and Egypt), external government debt is overwhelmingly to other governments or to international financial institutions (for example, the World Bank). Such debts are matters for government-to-government consultations; for political reasons none of the four debtors will be pushed too hard to pay old debts, and new credits will be made available as necessary to maintain political and economic stability. Such debts, in other words, are not in themselves a constraint on continuing deficits, nor does anybody worry about the risk associated with such debts. Governments giving foreign aid as loans to such debtor states for the most part already either publicly or privately accept that the loans are questionable if not bad. But since the desire to give foreign aid as loans to such countries is likely to continue, and since the governments of such countries appear willing to live with large foreign debts, one can confidently expect that aggregate, annual current-account deficits of from $3 to 5 billion will be placed with these four major debtors through the generosity of wealthy nations seeking political influence.

Aside from the chronic debtor states, the external public debts of several other major debtor nations have led to repayment difficulties in the 1970s. The governments of Peru, Chile, Zaire, and Turkey have all experienced problems in the 1970s in their efforts to increase their borrowing from private foreign sources, largely because of difficulties in making payments on already large outstanding government external debts. In the case of Peru, for example, U.S. banks in 1976 set conditions on a loan of $240 million, withholding the money until certain key policy changes had been announced by the Peruvian government. Chile was helped out of its debt difficulties by its official lenders, which postponed repayment obligations to themselves in 1974 and again in 1975; private foreign banks, which had not been included in the agreement to postpone repayments of old loans, were sufficiently encouraged by the improved financial position of the Chilean government to extend further loans. The decision to reschedule had been withheld by the U.S. government until after the fall of Allende; the position of the U.S. government as the major creditor was thus used to hurt Allende and to help Pinochet.

Nations with debt difficulties such as Peru, Zaire, Chile, and Turkey differ from the chronic debtors in that their governments have been able, at least intermittently, to maintain a better record of creditworthiness. Debt problems for such nations are often precipitated by a decline in export earnings or an uncontrolled increase in imports; if the situation looks bad, private foreign creditors will be unwilling to lend and the nation must go to official creditors for relief. Official creditors usually see the situation as needing some policy changes to reestablish sound fiscal management and take the opportunity to enforce such changes as conditions for official loans. The extent of policy change possible is always limited by the effect of such changes on the political stability of the regime in question. The United States, for example, can be expected to behave more leniently as a creditor to a friendly nation with a strategic location (such as Turkey) than to an unfriendly debtor (such as Chile under Allende) or a nation in which the United States does not feel there is a large political risk.

Among nations that have borrowed heavily since 1973, some of the developed countries (for example, Italy and Great Britain) have run into internal political problems resulting from the impact of deficits on domestic industrial activity, and some less developed countries (for example, Peru, Turkey, and Zaire) have had problems with private creditors who are unwilling to extend new loans in the face of large debt burdens. Most nations with large deficits, and even most nations with large external government debt (for example, Brazil and Mexico) have attracted some concern but have had little difficulty borrowing money. By 1978, with large U.S. deficits and shrunken OPEC surpluses, deficits and debt burdens had become much less worrisome than in 1974-76. But although the overall statistics look fine, there are several hidden difficulties. First, the growing importance of Japan and West Germany in international economic matters may sooner or later dilute the influence of the United States over debtor nations, making any level of debt more difficult to manage. Second, since 1973 much of the debt has been contracted with banks; the typical bank loan has a maturity of from three to seven years, shorter than the typical government-to-government loan which comprised a larger share of the debt before 1973. This means that loans have to be refinanced more frequently, leaving nations vulnerable to payment difficulties if for some reason they have trouble getting new loans.

NATIONS THAT PLAY THE ROLE OF
FINANCIAL INTERMEDIARY

When the price of oil went up in 1973, it quickly became apparent that some of the OPEC states could not spend all their income;

they had no choice but to invest abroad. It was also quickly apparent that some states would have to borrow to finance larger current-account deficits. But the neat juxtaposition of loanable funds and borrowing needs did not lead to loans from the OPEC surplus states to the deficit states. What has happened instead has been described in an internal document of the International Monetary Fund.

> In the period since 1974, there have been large inflows
> of foreign capital into the United States—including
> substantial amounts from the oil exporting countries—
> and these have had as their counterpart sizable out-
> flows of capital reflecting to a large extent the role of
> U.S. money and capital markets as intermediaries on
> an international scale. [9]

As described by the staff of the Senate Subcommittee on Foreign Economic Policy, the saving OPEC states have "interposed the commercial banks and international lending institutions as a buffer between themselves and the high risk borrowers." [10] For example, Citibank may receive a deposit in dollars from a Kuwaiti investor and, in turn, make a loan in dollars to the Brazilian government or to a company involved in Norwegian oil production. According to U.S. Treasury Department estimates, $49 billion was deposited by OPEC states in private commercial banks from 1974 to 1976, out of a total of $133 billion of OPEC foreign investments which could be identified (Table 5.4); there is a discrepancy of about $10 billion between identified OPEC investments and estimates of cumulative OPEC current-account surpluses for the three years. [11]

The role of U.S. banks as financial intermediaries is, of course, of interest to U.S. government officials charged with controlling the banking industry. In a statement submitted in 1977 to a House subcommittee studying the international operations of U.S. banks, Arthur Burns, chairman of the Board of Governors of the Federal Reserve System, recognized benefits to the U.S. banking industry from the inflow of OPEC money.

> [The OPEC states] largely avoided the route of extend-
> ing credit directly to the countries that were buyers of
> their oil, but instead funneled their huge surpluses
> into a variety of financial assets—chiefly bank deposits.
> They thereby shifted the banking opportunity—and with
> it, of course, the burden of credit evaluation—to others,
> which meant mainly the large American and European
> banks that the OPEC group used as depositories. [12]

TABLE 5.4

Estimated Disposition of OPEC Investable Surplus, 1974-76
($ billions)

	1974	1975	1976
United States	12.0	10.0	11.0
Short-term bank deposits,			
Treasury bills	9.3	0.3	0.3
Long-term bank deposits		0.8	0.3
U.S. Treasury bonds, notes	0.2	2.0	4.2
Other domestic bonds, notes	0.9	1.6	1.2
Equities	0.4	1.6	1.8
Subtotal: Banking and portfolio			
placements	10.8	6.3	7.8
Other (real estate, debt			
amortization, etc.)	1.2	3.7	3.2
Eurobanking market	22.5	8.0	10.5
United Kingdom	7.5	0.3	-1.0
Other developed countries	6.0	7.8	8.0
Less developed countries	4.0	6.0	6.0
Nonmarket countries	0.5	2.0	1.3
International financial institutions			
(including IMF oil facility)	3.8	4.3	1.8
Total allocated	56.3	38.3	37.5
Estimated cash surplus plus borrowings	59.0	40.0	42.0
Error of estimates of surplus and			
unidentified investments	2.8	1.8	4.5

Source: U.S. Congress, Senate, Committee on Foreign Re-
lations, Subcommittee on Foreign Economic Policy, International
Debt, the Banks, and U.S. Foreign Policy, 98th Cong., 1st sess.,
August 1977, p. 37.

    Banks, of course, have enjoyed mediating OPEC money flows.
As far as the big private banks were concerned, borrowing and
lending on a worldwide scale had already become business as usual
before 1973, but the post-1973 payments imbalances, including the
OPEC surpluses, vastly increased the sums involved. The effect of
the 1973 oil-price increases on the banking community was discussed
by C. Fred Bergsten, then Assistant Secretary for International

Affairs in the Treasury Department, before a House subcommittee in 1977: "Financial intermediation between lenders and borrowers, which . . . had already reached sizable international dimensions before 1973, has now become a central element in the world economy."[13] The effect of all the new business on the profits of the banks was, of course, favorable. In the words of the staff of the Senate Subcommittee on Foreign Economic Policy, "While the oil price increase was something close to a disaster for the world economy, it created a bonanza for the banks."[14]

The process of intermediation between OPEC surplus states with their savings and deficit states with their borrowing needs cannot, however, be reduced to the simple example given of one bank receiving a deposit and making a matching loan. A more complicated example would be as follows: the Saudi Arabian Monetary Authority buys $2 billion worth of U.S. government debt; investors in the United States who would have bought government debt if Saudi Arabia had not will have to shop around for other assets; interest rates will tend to fall with the presence of investors anxious to find some place to lend their money; with lower interest rates in U.S. capital markets, the Swedish government may decide to raise money by selling bonds in the United States or the government of South Korea may be encouraged to borrow from a consortium of U.S. banks. Intermediation in this example is provided by the U.S. capital market, but it is impossible to single out any specific institution that was responsible. OPEC investors bought some assets in the United States, and the United States somehow loaned money to some nonresident borrower.

According to U.S. Treasury Department estimates (given in Table 5.4), new OPEC investments in the United States came to $33 billion out of a total of $133 billion identified OPEC investments from 1974 to 1976. Such a figure, however, seriously understates the contribution of the OPEC states to U.S. financial power in the world, for the figure of $33 billion does not include OPEC deposits in foreign branches of U.S. banks.

U.S. banks abroad take part in what is known of as the "Eurocurrency market." This simply refers to the business of certain banks in accepting deposits and making loans in currencies other than the currency of the country in which the bank is located. For example, whenever a bank in West Germany (whether a U.S. branch or a West German bank) accepts a deposit in dollars or makes a loan in francs, that deposit or that loan is a part of the Eurocurrency market. The mix of currencies, locations, and bank nationalities is not, however, as much of a problem as it first appears to be: any deposit by OPEC investors in a branch of a U.S. bank anywhere in the world, no matter what currency the deposit is made in, may be counted as simply a deposit in a U.S. bank.

Estimates by the U.S. Treasury give OPEC Eurocurrency deposits of $41 billion for 1974-76. Estimates by Morgan Guaranty Trust for the end of 1977 give accumulated OPEC deposits in the Eurocurrency market of $54 billion; the total size of the market (net of double counting as a result of interbank loans) had reached an estimated $380 billion, growing at a rate of $60 to $70 billion annually. Thus, the OPEC contribution, although large, was only a part of the total market. [15]

It is generally accepted that much, if not most, of the OPEC Eurocurrency deposits have been placed in foreign branches of U.S. banks and in British banks; in Eurocurrency deposits as in other investments, OPEC investors have favored U.S. and British institutions. Because of recent experience with U.S. government regulations on foreign lending from banks resident in the United States, U.S. banks have conducted most of their foreign lending operations from bank branches outside of the United States; U.S. banks have naturally had an interest in directing new deposits by nonresidents into foreign rather than domestic branches so as to support their foreign lending operations. Moreover, foreign branches of U.S. banks have been able to offer higher rates of interest on dollar deposits than can be offered on dollar deposits by a bank branch located in the United States; in their Eurodollar operations (that is, in accepting dollar deposits) U.S. bank branches outside of the United States are not subject to interest controls as they would be in the United States but can pay depositors more for their money. Thus, there are several good reasons why OPEC deposits in U.S. banks have tended to show up in the Eurocurrency market rather than in the United States.

The role of the United States as financial intermediary for OPEC funds extends, however, beyond its use of the money invested directly in the United States and in U.S. banks abroad. OPEC states have also loaned money to the World Bank and to the International Monetary Fund. The World Bank borrows on bond markets and makes loans to developing countries for specific projects. The International Monetary Fund borrows directly from governments and makes foreign-currency loans directly to governments that are running short of foreign-currency reserves as part of a program to help such governments with their international financial problems. In both institutions, the World Bank and the IMF, nations vote according to a formula based on their contribution, but since the size of each nation's contribution seems to be based at least in part on international politics, the weight of each nation's vote reflects the ability of the various states to gain and hold influence in the organization. In the World Bank, the U.S. vote in 1976 was worth 23.19 percent of total votes against 5.03 percent for Japan and 6.47 percent for West Germany. In the International Monetary Fund, the

U.S. vote was worth 20.75 percent against 5.01 percent for West Germany and only 3.78 percent for Japan.[16] Fittingly, the head-quarters for both institutions are located in the heart of Washington, D.C., only blocks from the White House. OPEC loans to interna-tional financial institutions came to nearly $10 billion from 1974 to 1976; this total includes smaller contributions to other international financial institutions as well.

Flows of money from the saving OPEC states to the United States, to the foreign branches and subsidiaries of U.S. banks, and to U.S.-based international financial institutions contribute to the power and influence of the United States in its role as financial intermediary for other nations. But although the U.S. government apparently pursued the OPEC investments, and although U.S. bank-ers are clearly delighted doing business with the sheikhs, there are problems as well for the United States in the present situation. The role of intermediary exposes U.S. institutions to financial risks. In 1977, Representative John Cavanaugh, expressing concern over the security of present arrangements, asked for the U.S. govern-ment to put an end to the current system

> whereby the major U.S. banks provide the bulk of the
> lending to the oil importing countries of the world
> thereby imperiling their own solvency, the stability
> of the American banking system, the security of the
> American economy, and the future of the world
> monetary structure.[17]

But the risks to the United States in playing the role of finan-cial intermediary are better seen in political terms: lending through U.S. banks and bilateral government programs puts the United States in the position of creditor and collector. Although the offer of a loan encourages good relations, loans once made become debts, and burdensome levels of debt can weaken relations between two countries. This political danger has been well described by Senator Frank Church.

> What we are doing is making ourselves the fall guy. We
> are holding the bag. We are extending the loans. . . .
> I have never known very many debtors who love their
> creditors.
> Meanwhile, the OPEC countries over here who
> have created the whole problem are in Paris arm in
> arm with lesser developed countries condemning the
> western world. Our system seems to be conducive to
> produce just that effect.[18]

Concerns about the structure of international finance since 1973 have been widespread. The basis for the concern has been the necessity to place large deficits to balance OPEC surpluses. U.S. efforts to persuade Japan and West Germany to reduce their surpluses were largely unsuccessful through 1978, but in the meantime the surpluses of the OPEC nations have fallen to historically manageable levels. Nevertheless, financial and political risks—still exist for the United States as financial intermediary. Several courses of action have been offered to reduce the risks for the United States.

First, many observers have proposed that OPEC nations should make loans and credits directly available to the oil-importing deficit nations so that, as Representative Cavanaugh has argued, "the risk may reside where it appropriately belongs, not with the American people but with the OPEC exporters."[19]

This solution, however, seems impossible. OPEC investments would not be nearly as safe in many of the deficit countries in the world as they are in the United States or other major industrialized countries. More to the point, a loan by OPEC to a country such as Brazil, South Korea, or Zaire is not nearly as safe as a loan by the U.S. government or U.S. banks to the same country. The problem for OPEC is that its power is too narrow to enforce repayment on such nations. If any country which had accumulated large debts to OPEC nations demanded rescheduling or postponement of its repayments, OPEC nations would have to gain the support of other nations such as the United States to make any sanctions stick. Even an oil embargo would be impossible without the cooperation of the United States through its oil companies; witness the ability of Israel, South Africa, and Rhodesia to get oil despite efforts by key OPEC states to shut off their supplies. It is unlikely that the United States would support painful sanctions against nations in which it had important economic or political interests just for the sake of somebody else's loans. Thus, loans of OPEC funds to many countries in the world can only be safe if the loans are under the supervision of U.S. institutions or the institutions of some other major industrialized nation; and that is exactly the system which has been operating since 1973.

A second proposed method to reduce the risk inherent in the present expansion of international lending is that international financial institutions—and especially the International Monetary Fund—take a larger share of total lending to deficit nations. The larger role for the IMF would be designed to reduce the risk, though not so much the profits, for private banks. One of the Carter administration's key positive proposals to deal with the risk of intermediation has been just such an expansion of the International Monetary Fund. Plans to expand the IMF are discussed below.

Third, over the long run the question of how to reduce the risk to the United States from its international lending will most likely be resolved by curtailment of its role as financial intermediary. Such a curtailment is more or less inevitable with the emergence of Japan and West Germany as major economic powers. Not only will Japan and West Germany increase their international lending, but the presence of other trading blocs will reduce the influence that the United States can exercise over debtor nations, making it more difficult for U.S. institutions to make safe loans.

Since World War II, the possibility that nations might switch patrons, that is, realign themselves with different major trading nations, has been minimized by the narrow choice of possible patrons. The noncommunist nations were successfully organized into a single group by the United States, so that the only way out for a nation unhappy with its capitalist creditors was to turn to the Soviet Union. Such a step involved so many other economic and political matters that whatever external government debts that existed were hardly decisive by themselves.

With the emergence of Japan and West Germany as economic rivals to the United States, the choice of possible patrons has been widened. For a time at least, it is unlikely that the United States, Japan, or West Germany would undermine each other's international loans, but even so, rivalry over trade will have an effect on patterns of international lending.

The extension of a loan from one country to another is often related to exports from the lending country to the borrowing country. Money is loaned so that the debtor can buy the goods of the creditor. Thus, one would expect that over a period of years the major trading partner for a deficit nation would also become its major creditor. In years to come, the shares of international loans managed by West Germany and Japan are likely to rise toward parity with the United States, as befits their large and growing shares of world trade.

Outstanding international debts act as a restraint on current imports for debtor nations. If outstanding debts are owed to some country other than the major trading partner, strong incentives exist on the part of both the debtor nation and the major trading partner to try to get around the constraints of outstanding debt. As the major creditor to the less developed countries, the United States could easily find itself in an exposed position, working for repayment against the interests of other industrial nations as well as against the interests of the less developed countries.

PRIVATE BANKS AND THE INTERNATIONAL
MONETARY FUND

Private banks and bond markets have managed most of the
international lending necessary to finance the large-current-account
deficits of the post-1973 period. According to Treasury Department
estimates, an aggregate total of $225 billion of international loans
were needed by deficit nations from 1974 to 1976 to help them pay
their international bills. Seventy-five percent of this total, or $170
billion, was provided by private capital markets, much of it through
private banks. Of the remaining 25 percent, 7 percent, or $15 bil-
lion, was provided by the International Monetary Fund, and 18 percent, or about $40 billion, was provided by other official sources
(governments, the World Bank, and so on).[20]

Stimulated by OPEC deposits and the large volume of new
lending to help finance current-account deficits, international banks
expanded their external claims on "nonbanks" (claims on nonresidents of the country where the bank's home office is located, not
counting bank-to-bank loans) from $154 billion in 1973 to $326 billion in 1976. Much of this new lending was accounted for by loans
to developed countries, but a large share involved bank loans to
governments and businesses in the less developed nations. The
share of U.S. banks in total lending ranged from 36 to 38 percent
from 1973 to 1976.[21]

From the point of view of governments of the non-oil less
developed countries as a group, an increasingly large share of their
external debt has come to be held by banks in the developed countries rather than by other governments or official lenders (such as
the World Bank). This shift to private market financing was already
underway in the early 1970s as the U.S. government, under the
leadership of a Republican administration, held down the U.S. contribution to the World Bank and other regional development banks
and also restrained the volume of U.S. government loans. According to IMF data, private commercial banks increased their share of
the external debt of governments of non-oil less developed countries
from about 7 percent in 1970 to nearly 27 percent in 1976.[22]

The shift from official lending to private lending has affected
the amount of loans flowing to various countries. Banks loan for
profit not aid; U.S. government loans go, for example, to India,
Bangladesh, Egypt, and other needy or politically important nations,
while private banks loan according to the security provided by each

country; to a banker security is mostly a matter of the expectation of strong future export performance. Among the group of non-oil less developed countries most bank-to-government loans have gone to a handful of nations. Brazil and Mexico alone have each had as much as a quarter or more of outstanding bank debt for all non-oil less developed countries in recent years. Another group of nations, Argentina, Peru, South Korea, Zaire, and South Africa, has brought the share for major borrowers to approximately two-thirds that of all non-oil less developed countries together (omitting bank borrowing by governments of more advanced Mediterranean countries such as Greece and Spain, countries which are listed in World Bank data along with the less developed countries. In addition, several OPEC countries (especially Algeria and Indonesia) have demonstrated an ability to spend all they earn as well as to pile up international bank debts. U.S. banks have managed much of the lending to governments and other customers in the less developed countries. Most of the handful of major debtor countries among these countries have had especially strong ties with U.S. business and have depended on loans from U.S. banks.

The role of private banks in providing much of the borrowing to cover post-1973 deficits was absolutely essential—and more or less inevitable—given the inability and unwillingness of governments and other official lending agencies to respond with massive new loans in a short period of time. While there has been some exaltation over the flexibility and performance of private capital markets, many people have had difficulty trusting the stability of a system with massive and mounting international lending by private banks, much of it to foreign governments. In early 1977, Chairman Burns of the Federal Reserve System testified to the Senate Banking Committee that although he had heard a lot of talk about "the wonderful performance of the private banking system," he remained skeptical: "What was happening was simply that the loans were piling up as the surpluses grew. The banks got the money and the banks extended the loans. But this couldn't go on."[23]

Aside from private banks and bond markets, the only other major source of international credit that has increased its share of international loans outstanding is the International Monetary Fund. At the end of 1973, IMF claims on governments around the world totaled only $1 billion. By mid-1977 this sum had grown to over $14 billion. IMF loans to non-oil less developed countries grew during that period from $939 million to $5.3 billion, increasing the IMF's share of the external debt of those governments from 1.6 percent in 1973 to about 4 percent in 1977. Despite this large increase in the IMF's share of international lending, the Carter administration, along with large private banks, has been arguing

that the IMF is "too small" for what it has to do. In 1978, under
U.S. leadership, the IMF increased the contributions of its members by an aggregate of over $20 billion, and moves were initiated
to add another $25 billion within the next several years.

According to its original design, drawn up in 1944 under the
direction of the United States, the task of the IMF was to restrain
unreasonable current-account surpluses and deficits among the member nations and to limit government interference in international
flows of trade and capital. The specter that haunted economic planners in 1944 as they set up the IMF was that of the major trading
nations devaluing, pushing exports, shutting out imports, and leading the world into depression in the 1930s. Those who designed the
IMF, therefore, were concerned about potential disagreements among
major trading nations; thus, in the design of the IMF member governments contributed money according to assigned quotas and were
able to borrow, vote on each other's loans, and vote on other matters according to those same quotas. The IMF, in other words, was
given the character of a "rich man's" U.N., and this is entirely
appropriate to the focus of its designed task, which is to coordinate
the international economic policies of the rich nations.

Nevertheless, the assigned task of coordinating policies among
the rich nations is no longer—if it has ever been—a central feature
of IMF operations, despite its design. Instead, the IMF has built a
strong tradition of using its loans to influence the economic policies
of governments of less wealthy nations in need of foreign exchange.
The central feature of IMF lending is that large loans (that is, large
in relation to a nation's quota) are tied to conditions; in a typical
program, the borrowing government is enjoined to limit budget
deficits, to change certain wage and price policies, and to maintain
conditions of free trade and currency exchange. From 1973 to 1975,
for example, 18 different countries were given large loans with conditions; these included 15 less developed countries along with Finland, Italy, and Israel. But while the focus of its operations has
come to rest on the less developed countries and on the less wealthy
developed countries, the IMF retains the character of a rich man's
U.N., with votes on all loans allocated in a rough way according to
the wealth of each member nation. Robert Aliber, professor in the
graduate school of business at the University of Chicago, has clearly
stated this interpretation of IMF operations.

> Increasingly one has the feeling that the Fund is a ve-
> hicle by which the larger industrial countries set rules
> of behaviour for the smaller countries in the system.
> The larger industrial countries are almost outside the
> scope of the Fund in their behaviour toward each other. [24]

Since 1973, changing conditions in international trade and finance have raised the issue of the appropriate role of the IMF. These changing conditions include, first, the large volume of balancing deficits necessary for other nations, especially from 1974 to 1977, in the face of large surpluses by OPEC nations and by Japan and West Germany, and, second, the rapid expansion of international lending by private banks, particularly to governments of less developed countries. These new developments posed a problem: private banks have felt increasingly exposed and unsure of the security of further loans as their share of government debt has increased. Although the problem of balancing deficits seems to have been solved by 1978 with the reduction of OPEC surpluses, U.S. bankers and government officials have continued to argue that the risks of increased bank lending to less developed countries warranted a larger, if not explicitly redefined role, for the International Monetary Fund. They have insistently proposed that the IMF use its multilateral stature, its lending power, and its influence over the policies of member nations to help the banks continue their loans to debtor nations.

In a 1977 international conference on monetary matters, Secretary of the Treasury Michael Blumenthal called for careful study of the "possibilities of developing a closer interaction, a smoother transition, between financing through the private market and official financing through the IMF."[25] Although Blumenthal made a number of specific proposals—for example, that the IMF share its confidential information on a government with banks considering loans to that government—such formal links are hardly necessary for a high degree of partnership to develop between the IMF and the private banks.

There are several ways in which the IMF has operated in recent years so as to support larger levels of bank loans to debtor governments. First, the IMF stands ready with potential loans should any government get in trouble with its bank creditors, and second, the IMF makes loans contingent in such a way as to reassure banks that the government concerned is responsible and creditworthy.

Although the international debts of governments should be considered long term in most cases, the typical private bank loan is for a period of from three to seven years. When any loan comes due, political and economic conditions in the country are evaluated, and if the situation looks favorable, the loan is refunded, or "rolled over." If, on the other hand, conditions do not look good, private banks are hesitant to make new loans, but without new loans the government would almost surely find itself unable to maintain payments on old debts. The possibility of this happening at some time in the future is always a restraint on current loans, but the existence of the IMF, with its potential to lend to nations that are facing difficulties with their commercial creditors, serves to reassure bankers that their loans will somehow be repaid. As Richard Cooper, State Department Undersecretary for Economic Affairs, has explained, "Official financing has an important psychological factor. . . . There is a perceived need for official backstopping of the financial system." Cooper went on to argue that in order to encourage further lending by private banks, the IMF needed more money "so as to reassure all that a source of official finance exists on a scale which is sufficient to cope with whatever financial turbulence we may encounter in the next several years."[26]

When private banks are hesitant to continue lending to a specific debtor government and the IMF finds it necessary or prudent to step in with its own loans, the conditions attached to IMF lending serve in general to restore the faith of the banking community in the policies and prospects of the debtor government. Large IMF loans are released in stages, dependent on the performance of the borrowing country in meeting the IMF's conditions; these staged loans are known as "stand-by agreements." Anthony Solomon, Undersecretary for Monetary Affairs of the Treasury Department, explained the relation of stand-by agreements to bank lending as follows:

> Typically, when the Fund reaches an agreement with a country, the banks, instead of rushing to ask for their own money because the IMF has put some money in, are willing to increase their lending to the country because it has entered a period of stabilization under the tight control of the IMF. . . . The very fact that they are meeting the IMF's performance criteria and thus continue to be eligible to draw from the IMF's drawings . . . tends to represent a kind of Good Housekeeping seal of approval. Good performance under an IMF program tends to result in private capital markets, private banks being willing to lend more to the country concerned.[27]

The IMF thus works with the banks in two ways: it backstops private banks when governments appear unable to maintain payments on their outstanding bank debt, and it uses its own lending power to encourage sound financial practices by debtor governments and, hence, to encourage more bank loans. A larger IMF with more money to lend would obviously be more reassuring. In arguing for Congress to vote more money for the IMF, Anthony Solomon noted in particular that more money for the IMF "is expected to encourage banks to continue to expand their foreign lending."[28]

Even without the Blumenthal plan for explicit cooperation between the IMF and private banks, the IMF has taken the role of supporting the banks in their lending to debtor governments. Such a role erodes the authority and impartial character of the IMF, identifying it more and more as the agent of the rich in the affairs of the poor.

Whenever a debtor government finds difficulty maintaining payments of interest and principle on its external debt, the problem immediately becomes political in both a domestic and an international sense. If the IMF is asked for a loan, the conditions of that loan typically involve matters of interest in the domestic political struggles of the nation in question. In making its loans conditional on certain economic policies, the IMF finds itself allied with some domestic political groups against the interests of others.

Confrontations between the ruling government and opposition groups, for example, are often precipitated by the IMF's insistence on wage restraints and the withdrawal of government subsidies on urban food supplies. In the context of an underdeveloped society, it can be argued that such policies hurt particularly the urban middle class and those in the government bureaucracy and are thus reasonable both for social equity as well as fiscal austerity; but the "correctness" or "benevolence" of the IMF's influence on the debtor government does not defuse the political tensions created by such interference. To seek greater interference in the domestic affairs of other nations is a dangerous course for the IMF to take, no matter how valuable its advice or how necessary the policies it pushes on the borrowing government.

PROBLEMS FOR THE UNITED STATES AS FINANCIAL INTERMEDIARY

As the most important intermediary in international finance, the United States is the nation most acutely sensitive to the risks of the present debt build-up. Attention commonly focuses on financial risks, but the more serious risks are political.

The financial risk is that a debtor government may not be able to pay its loans to private banks when the loans come due. Scenarios of financial disaster beginning at this point tell a story that goes from debt default through bank failure to economic collapse. Although repayment difficulties are likely to occur in the future, as in the past, at the rate of several countries every five years, none of the rest of the scenario is realistic. First, the sums involved in all but a few countries are not large enough to seriously damage the big banks that are in the forefront in international lending operations.

And second, even if a debtor government found itself unable to pay, the loan would not be written off; repayments would be rescheduled with interest so that the banks would eventually recover their loans. A nation could effectively repudiate its debts only by breaking off most if not all of its economic relations with the United States; this occurs much less frequently, however, than rescheduling operations and, furthermore, it seldom occurs entirely without warning.

The political risk of international debt is that onerous repayment obligations may weaken friendly governments and damage relations between creditor and debtor nations. As a creditor, the United States has often used restraint with nations which find themselves with difficulties meeting their debt obligations. Good relations come first, before repayment. Fear of the political risk also leads the United States as creditor to attempt to keep debt obligations within reasonable limits so as not to create a situation in which the burden of debt repayment becomes a destructive political issue.

The staff of the Senate Subcommittee on Foreign Economic Policy expressed concern about the political risks to the United States in the post-1973 debt and deficit problems of a number of nations.

> There is every reason, therefore, for the U.S. government to be concerned about the present debt buildup, not only because of the large exposure of American banks, but also for its broader foreign policy implications. The financial problems of major allies such as Italy or France are naturally given high priority attention in Washington. But the United States also has important security interests in other debtor countries, such as Turkey, Greece, and, to a lesser extent, in Zaire. It can hardly afford to stand by and watch the economies of these countries collapse, or to have their governments undermined politically by financial difficulties. [29]

The best way to restrain the political risks of international debt is to reduce current-account deficits for major debtors whenever possible. But with large OPEC, Japanese, and West German surpluses during the middle 1970s, that option was difficult to follow. Instead, the U.S. government followed a policy of attempting to spread the deficits as widely as possible and to support banks in further lending operations. Such temporizing solutions were intended to last until OPEC current-account surpluses receded; by late 1978, with projected current-account surpluses for OPEC nations of around $11 billion for 1978, the worst problems associated with payment imbalances seem to have passed.

NOTES

1. U.S. Congress, Senate, Committee on Foreign Relations, Bretton Woods Agreements Amendments Act of 1977, 95th Cong., 1st sess., November 15, 1977.

2. International Monetary Fund, International Financial Statistics, 30, 11 (Washington, D.C.: IMF, November 1977), pp. 304-5, 377.

3. U.S. Congress, Senate, Committee on Foreign Relations, Subcommittee on Foreign Economic Policy, International Debt, the Banks, and U.S. Foreign Policy (staff report), 95th Cong., 1st sess., August 1977, p. 37.

4. U.S. Congress, Senate, Committee on Banking, Housing and Urban Affairs, The Middle East: 1976 (Report by Senator Adlai E. Stevenson), 94th Cong., 2d sess., April 1976, p. 6.

5. International Debt, the Banks, and U.S. Foreign Policy, p. 31.

6. Gerald Pollack, "The Economic Consequences of the Energy Crisis," The World Economic Crisis, ed. William Bundy (New York: Norton, 1975), p. 126.

7. OPEC investors in 1976 exchanged some of their sterling holdings for other currencies. This contributed to the fall of the pound, but since the United Kingdom was concerned at the time to reduce its trade deficit and wanted to devalue, the effect on the pound of OPEC nations' selling their pound investments cannot be used as evidence of uncooperative behavior. In any case, OPEC nations could (and probably did) continue to make large deposits in British banks; the deposits would simply be denominated in dollars and would be listed as investments in the Eurocurrency market rather than in the United Kingdom.

8. Testimony of Paul Watson, in U.S. Congress, Senate, Committee on Banking, Housing and Urban Affairs, Subcommittee on International Finance, International Debt, 95th Cong., 1st sess., August 30, 1977, p. 199. Watson cites: Gordon W. Smith, "The External Debt Prospects of the Non-Oil-Exporting Developing Countries" (Washington, D.C.: Overseas Development Council, 1977).

9. International Monetary Fund, "World Economic Outlook—General Survey" (Washington, D.C.: IMF, June 1977), p. 21.

10. International Debt, the Banks, and U.S. Foreign Policy, p. 5.

11. Ibid., p. 4.

12. U.S. Congress, House, Committee on Banking, Finance and Urban Affairs, Subcommittee on Financial Institutions Supervision, Regulation and Insurance, International Banking Operations, 95th Cong., 1st sess., March and April, 1977, p. 61.

13. Testimony of C. Fred Bergsten, in U.S. Congress, House, Committee on Banking, Finance and Urban Affairs, Subcommittee on Financial Institutions Supervision, Regulations and Insurance, International Banking Operations, 95th Cong., 1st sess., March and April 1977, p. 548.

14. International Debt, the Banks, and U.S. Foreign Policy, p. 3.

15. Morgan Guaranty, "World Financial Markets July 1978," taken from: Andrew Liddell, "Lean times ahead since lending is for borrowers," Far Eastern Economic Review, September 22, 1978, p. 41.

16. Voting shares in the World Bank are taken from: World Bank, Annual Report, 1977 (Washington, D.C.: World Bank, 1977), p. 150. Voting shares in the International Monetary Fund are from: U.S. Congress, House, Committee on Banking, Currency and Housing, Amendment of the Articles of Agreement and Increase in Quotas of the International Monetary Fund (Communication from the Secretary of the Treasury), 94th Cong., 2d sess., April 9, 1976, p. 4 and App. B, p. 13.

17. John J. Cavanaugh, "Statement Before the House Banking Committee on H.R. 9214" (Washington, D.C.: Congress, Office of Representative John J. Cavanaugh, November 29, 1977), p. 11.

18. Frank Church, quoted in Cavanaugh, pp. 10-11.

19. Cavanaugh, p. 11.

20. Testimony of Anthony Solomon, in U.S. Congress, Senate, Committee on Banking, Housing and Urban Affairs, Subcommittee on International Finance, International Debt, 95th Cong., 1st sess., August 29, 1977, p. 27.

21. International Debt, the Banks, and U.S. Foreign Policy, p. 44.

22. International Monetary Fund, Annual Report 1977 (Washington, D.C.: IMF, 1977), p. 3.

23. Arthur Burns, quoted in Cavanaugh, p. 3.

24. Testimony of Robert Z. Aliber, in U.S. Congress, House, Committee on Banking, Finance and Urban Affairs, Subcommittee on International Trade, Investment and Monetary Policy, U.S. Participation in the Supplementary Financing Facility of the International Monetary Fund, 95th Cong., 1st sess., September 29, 1977, p. 190.

25. Michael Blumenthal, "Toward International Equilibrium: A New Strategy for the Longer Pull" (paper delivered at the International Monetary Conference, Tokyo, May 25, 1977), (Washington, D.C.: U.S. Treasury Department, May 24, 1977), p. 8.

26. Testimony of Richard Cooper, in U.S. Congress, House, Committee on Banking, Finance and Urban Affairs, Subcommittee

on International Trade, Investment and Monetary Policy, U.S. Participation in the Supplementary Financing Facility of the International Monetary Fund, 95th Cong., 1st sess., September 20, 1977, p. 29.

27. Testimony of Anthony Solomon, in U.S. Congress, House, Committee on Banking, Finance and Urban Affairs, Subcommittee on International Trade, Investment and Monetary Policy, U.S. Participation in the Supplementary Financing Facility of the International Monetary Fund, 95th Cong., 1st sess., September 20, 1977, p. 72.

28. Ibid., p. 12.

29. International Debt, the Banks, and U.S. Foreign Policy, p. 7.

6

THE CONTINUING STRUGGLE FOR
ENERGY AND ECONOMIC POWER

During 1978 several developments occurred marking the success of the policy of high oil prices. First, the OPEC current-account surplus declined to historically sustainable levels—from nearly $30 billion in 1977 to about $11 billion in 1978. Second, the OPEC nations began another series of stiff price increases for their oil exports. And third, the U.S. dollar was devalued against the yen and the deutsche mark. These three developments have a logical relationship if seen in terms of the arguments of the first five chapters of this book. The decline of OPEC current-account surpluses relieved the need for balancing deficits for other countries. Since placing balancing deficits had been a problem from 1973 to 1977, the decline in OPEC surpluses removed a major obstacle to higher prices, and higher prices followed. Moreover, the need for large U.S. current-account deficits to keep the pressure of balancing deficits off weaker and smaller economies had also passed. Consequently, the United States was able to devalue as part of an effort to reduce its current-account deficit without having to worry so much about the effect of such actions on the current-account balances of its trading partners. Thus, by the end of 1978 the powers that control oil had achieved complete success in their policy to attain a new price plateau, a policy which had seemed so astounding in 1973.

Toward the end of 1978 successful adjustment to the higher prices represented a clear victory for the United States at the expense of West Germany and Japan. But the struggle over oil and energy and, in broader terms, over international economic power continues. In this chapter, four topics of continuing interest will be discussed briefly in the context of the arguments which have already been presented in Chapters 1 through 5.

First, although high prices have been well established, questions remain concerning the future of the international oil cartel. In the late 1970s, Mexico and China began to emerge as major new sources of oil for world markets. Even before these new sources

had begun to produce near capacity, OPEC nations were bothered in
1977 and early 1978 with excess oil. In addition to these challenges
to the cartel's control of oil, important nations outside the cartel
have been working to weaken ties between the United States and its
key OPEC allies. The cartel, however, is very firmly constructed;
its staying power is based in large part on the strength of the United
States. Accordingly, the demise of the cartel would be associated
not so much with a reduction in world oil prices but with a sharp
weakening of the U.S. position in world affairs.

Second, the large size of the U.S. oil-import bill continues to
be used without too much effect as one argument for an effective U.S.
energy program. The United States has the most profligate energy
habits of all major industrial nations; despite being one of the three
largest oil producers in the world, the United States also imports
more oil than any other nation. Oil-import bills of $41.1 and $38.6
billion in 1977 and 1978, respectively, have exceeded the U.S.
current-account deficits in these years[1] and have been clearly linked
to the weakening of the dollar. Nevertheless, a strong argument can
be made that the international economic consequences of the United
States' thirst for foreign oil are beneficial rather than harmful for
the United States. From a strictly chauvinistic point of view, the
case for a domestic energy program based on international economic
considerations is not strong.

Third, although the United States has played since World War II
the largest role in controlling the flow of oil to Western Europe and
Japan, the Soviet Union and China have parts to play as well. The
Soviet Union, with the potential to be a major oil exporter, has been
concerned, like the United States, with the emerging power of West
Germany and Japan. Without the massive oil reserves of the Soviet
Union, China has nevertheless made moves to expand its oil exports
and has benefited both politically and economically from Japan's
search for oil security in the 1970s. Thus, for economic and politi-
cal reasons none of the three continental strategic powers—the United
States, the Soviet Union, and China—is likely to favor cheap and
plentiful oil for the two oil-poor economic powers—Japan and West
Germany.

Fourth, the oil crisis of the 1970s has heightened political
awareness in Japan and West Germany about the security of all their
foreign resource supplies. Both countries have responded with intensified efforts to gain influence over resources throughout the
world. Competition between the United States, Japan, and West
Germany for resources could mean an improved bargaining position
for Third World nations, but could also lead to attempts at subversion, control, and political repression to promote and to defend the
economic interests of the various industrial powers.

Overall, the events of the 1970s have accelerated the trend toward politicization of international economic relationships. Such an observation serves at once as a summary of this study and as a prognosis for the future.

THE FUTURE OF THE CARTEL

Close relations between the U.S. government and most of the key OPEC states are the central feature of the oil cartel in the 1970s. Hence, the future of the cartel is a matter of international politics involving the fortunes of the United States against those of the Soviet Union, Western Europe, and Japan. Although the political coloring of the cartel may change through coups and revolutions in the oil-exporting countries, the policy of high and higher prices is not likely to be rescinded.

In 1974 prominent Americans publicly debated the option of invading OPEC nations to bring down the price of oil. The speculation was absurd for several reasons, not the least of which was the fact that the nations involved were essentially allies following the wishes of the U.S. government. But such speculations were misleading in another respect: the United States deals not so much with OPEC nations as with more or less narrow oligarchic elites at the helm of the various OPEC governments. Exercise of U.S. influence is much more readily managed through persuasion, political and financial manipulation, and, if necessary and if conditions permit, a coup. These levers of control are available to others as well: in future years coups and struggles for power within the various OPEC countries will give the best opportunities for outsiders to establish their influence over the oil-exporting policies of the various OPEC states.

As discussed in Chapter 5, only a few of the OPEC states have consistently saved a large share of their post-1973 oil revenues. Other OPEC nations, such as Indonesia, Venezuela, Nigeria, and Algeria have quickly adjusted their spending patterns to absorb the higher revenues; a drop in oil prices or even the failure of oil prices to adjust to inflation and to the fall of the dollar in foreign exchange markets would threaten the ability of such nations to maintain current levels of spending. Many of the OPEC nations, therefore, had become dependent soon after 1973 on the maintenance of a high price level for their economic and even political stability. In future years, whatever foreign power attempts to maintain or to gain influence over the governments of such nations will have no chance of keeping its clique in power unless high oil prices are maintained.

Those OPEC nations that do not spend their revenues add strength to the cartel in a different way. Saudi Arabia, Kuwait, and the United Arab Emirates have received since 1973 more oil income than they could reasonably spend. For such countries, oil output is elastic: if a cutback is necessary to scale output to demand, their import programs are not affected at all. The level of output is an administrative decision with insignificant internal economic consequences. In response to strenuous conservation efforts by Western European nations and Japan or new output from the North Sea, China, Mexico, and Alaska, these cartel countries are able to adjust production temporarily until economic growth makes up the difference.

The most significant and realistic threats to U.S. influence in the various cartel nations are related to the desires of various Western European nations and Japan to improve their position vis-à-vis the United States. So far, the most successful and forward nation in its attempts to disrupt the cartel has been France, which in 1978 and 1979 played a part in Iran by, for example, providing Ayatollah Khomeini with a home-in-exile. West Germany and Japan have been attempting to increase their influence in various OPEC nations through trade.

For any of the nations of Western Europe, the oil production of any of a half dozen OPEC nations would be sufficient to cover all their oil needs; there is at least the possibility that West Germany, for example, could satisfy its oil needs with one key oil-exporting ally. Japan, which imports more oil than all but two OPEC nations (Saudi Arabia and Iran) are able to export, has very little hope in the near future of escaping from substantial reliance on the U.S.-dominated cartel.

Since the Soviet Union does not need foreign oil, even if it were to gain influence in an OPEC country it would have to make arrangements to have the oil sold to a Western European country or to Japan. Thus, even if the Soviet Union were to be involved in upsetting the cartel in one or more exporting countries, an important oil-importing country would have to be involved as well. Whichever oil-importing country was involved would be risking the displeasure of the United States and possibly even interruption of some of its other oil imports.

The core of U.S. control of oil is, of course, represented by Saudi Arabia, which has the largest known reserves in the world and a production capacity that is somewhere over a third of total OPEC oil exports. But the resilient strength of the cartel is provided most of all by the cartel's ability to coordinate the production of a number of oil exporters to provide a relatively secure supply of energy to the oil-importing nations. When in 1978 Iran with a sixth of OPEC exports shut down completely, alternative sources of oil were readily at hand to continue the flow of oil to Western Europe and Japan. The security provided by such a multicountry back-up system is an important feature keeping the oil-importing nations from seeking private accommodations with one or two separate oil exporters.

In sum, the cartel's price structure is secure. The macro-economic problem of balancing deficits has been solved. And a lower price would be so unsettling to many of the OPEC nations that domestic political instability would discredit whatever local leadership group and whatever foreign government was responsible for endorsing the lower prices. Furthermore, the position of the United States in the center of the international oil trade seems secure as well; unfriendly or uncooperative governments in one or more of the major OPEC countries, with the exception of Saudi Arabia, which is crucial to U.S. influence in oil, can more or less easily be accommodated without disrupting the multinational framework of U.S. control.

U.S. OIL IMPORTS AS AN ARGUMENT FOR AN ENERGY PROGRAM

By all accounts, the United States has been one of the most profligate consumers of energy in the world. During the 1970s, the United States has consumed about three times as much energy per capita as Japan and about twice as much as West Germany. Even in terms of energy consumption per dollar of GNP, the rate of U.S. energy consumption has far exceeded that of either Japan or West Germany. In 1974, for example, the United States consumed energy at the rate of 1.72 kilograms of coal equivalent per dollar of GNP against .93 kilograms of coal equivalent per dollar of GNP for both Japan and West Germany.[2]

As discussed in the first five chapters, Japan and West Germany have taken offense at the energy gluttony of the United States and have attempted through trade policies and negotiations to persuade the United States to undertake efforts to conserve and to develop alternative forms of energy. Since all three nations import oil from the same group of oil exporters, their interests as oil consumers are competitive.

Despite widespread publicity related to the oil crisis, U.S. domestic energy policies have been notoriously weak and ineffective in curbing consumption. That the United States has not restrained its oil consumption since 1973 to the same extent as have the already more energy efficient economies of Japan and West Germany has exposed the U.S. government to domestic and foreign criticism for not being able to act effectively in the face of the energy crisis.

One common argument for a U.S. energy program has been based on the ballooning size of the U.S. oil-import bill, which has risen from less than $3 billion in 1970 to over $40 billion in 1977 and promises to go higher. Large oil bills have been held responsible for the trade and current-account deficits experienced by the United States in the late 1970s. The deficits, in turn, have severely weakened the dollar; between January and October 1978, for example, the value of a U.S. dollar fell from 240 yen to 180 yen in foreign exchange markets. Representatives of the governments of Japan and West Germany have been particularly insistent on the relationship between the large U.S. oil-import bill and the problems of the U.S. economy.

Although the oil-import bill is most often seen as a burden, there is a way in which large oil-import bills benefit the United States as well. Imports of $40 billion worth of oil serve in a sense to justify exports of $40 billion worth of other commodities to pay for the oil. Such exports represent jobs and profits in U.S. industry. The weakening of the dollar, which is associated with the massive U.S. oil-import bill, is, contrary to much rhetoric, favorable to the U.S. economy. With a cheaper dollar, U.S. goods are given a competitive advantage in world markets, and U.S. exports are promoted. Since the key to world economic power is found in shares of world export trade and not the success or failure of the various currencies to hold their values against each other, a falling dollar in the context of the late 1970s represents an advance of U.S. economic power at the expense of West Germany and Japan. In support of such an interpretation, the governments of West Germany and Japan have repeatedly expressed their concern over the falling value of the dollar.

The fear of growing dependence on foreign energy supplies has also been a theme in calls to reduce U.S. oil imports through an effective energy program. Fears of an oil cutoff must be put in perspective: the power of the United States in world affairs is so crucially involved in control over international oil that the risk of a serious politically motivated cutoff of oil to the United States is equivalent to the risk of the collapse of U.S. power in the world. Consequently, worries over energy dependence for the United States are next to superfluous. Moreover, the large volume of U.S. oil imports supports the role of the U.S. government and oil companies in organizing and supervising international flows of oil.

Thus, on closer examination, the case for a U.S. energy program based on the size of the oil-import bills and the volume of oil imports is weakened by strong counterarguments. Although the cost of oil imports to the U.S. economy is large, there are reasons why the United States may be willing and able to continue such imports indefinitely. Oil-import bills weaken the dollar and thereby support the efforts of U.S. exporters to maintain their shares of world markets. And the share of U.S. oil imports in world oil trade contributes to U.S. influence in oil more than it represents any risk to U.S. energy supplies. From a strictly chauvinistic point of view, the case for a U.S. energy program to cut oil imports looks very weak.

A better case for curtailing U.S. energy imports can be made from an internationalist position, that is, that such imports upset the rest of the world. One good example of such an argument has been given by Carroll L. Wilson.

> On any rational look at the production and consumption of energy all over the world, the United States represents not only a statistical discrepancy and target for villain (six percent consuming 33 percent, and getting greater), but a potential disruptive force in almost every market day by day; only if this is brought under control can the United States play any responsible role in the effort that may have to be undertaken within the next decade, or at least by the end of the century—to balance and distribute world energy supplies much more fairly and reasonably than nature or men have ever done to date. [3]

The internationalist case is not, however, entirely convincing. A fair and reasonable distribution of energy in the world would by all accounts involve a drastic program of conservation in the United States. The big winners from any U.S. program of conservation would, however, be Western Europe and Japan. Whether the United States improves the prospects for peace and stability in the world by hurting itself in order to help Western Europe and Japan is not clear. The U.S. share of world oil consumption was larger in the 1950s and 1960s than in the 1970s; there is no logical reason why a large share of world energy for the United States will be more unsettling in the 1980s than before. Indeed, one can almost argue the opposite: any moves to share energy more equitably with Japan and West Germany will merely help them to grow to a level where their challenge to U.S. leadership and U.S. stewardship of world oil is more unsettling than it is at present. The situation of the past and present, in which world power and world energy supplies are not fairly distributed, may be better for stability and peace than would equitable access to energy.

In any case, the internationalist case for a domestic U.S. energy program—that fair play in oil by the United States will encourage cooperation, good will, and peace among the major industrial powers and throughout the world—carries little weight in the United States. Congress and the president would have a tough job trying to convince voters as well as themselves that a stiff domestic price increase for gasoline, for example, was necessary to give West Germany and Japan better access to world oil supplies.

Arguments for a U.S. energy program based on the weight of the oil-import bill, the risk of energy dependence, or a sense of fair play for other oil-importing nations have not been successful in bringing in a rigorous energy program and are not likely to be. The need for a U.S. energy program based on such considerations is neither clear nor strong enough to move the U.S. government, including Congress, to take the painful steps that would be necessary for an effective reduction in U.S. oil consumption. For at least the present, the United States is strong enough to pay for oil, to protect its foreign oil supplies, and to weather the resentments of other countries forced into drastic energy conservation programs. By the time the United States is finally forced by such considerations to curtail its oil imports, it will have already lost a large measure of its power in the world.

A case for conservation can, however, be made on environmental grounds. Since the future promises abundant energy from the sun, from various nuclear processes, and from other sources, the environmental argument will sooner or later provide the only effective and necessary constraint. Energy and what people do with energy are basic to the continuing process of environmental destruction. Despite the intensively discussed energy crisis of the 1970s and the anticipated exhaustion of world oil supplies within the next few generations, a more basic problem for the continuation of civilization as we know it will be the destructive effects of too much energy, not any energy shortage.

Aside from the environmental argument, which is sufficient in itself, there are no compelling reasons why the United States needs a rigorous energy program. Unfortunately, those energy programs which have been introduced to cut down on oil imports have often promoted such environmentally destructive policies as increased coal burning, strip mining, and offshore oil drilling for their effect in reducing U.S. oil imports.

THE SOVIET UNION, CHINA, AND THE OIL CARTEL

Like the United States, both the Soviet Union and China are continental strategic powers with domestic resources of energy sufficient to support advanced industrial society. The two other key centers of economic power, West Germany and Japan, are militarily weak and dependent on imports of energy to maintain their industrial activities. With their military power and their domestic oil resources, each of the three continental strategic powers is able to exercise some degree of influence over the oil supplies of Japan and West Germany. For their own reasons, both the Soviet Union and China apparently find themselves on the same side as the United States, favoring high oil prices for Western Europe and Japan.

Parallels between the oil industries of the United States and the Soviet Union are striking: domestic production began at about the same time in the nineteenth century in both countries, the volumes of production were roughly equivalent for a number of years until the turn of the century, and the volumes of production were again roughly equivalent in the early 1970s. Oil reserves for the Soviet Union are, however, much greater than those of the United States; with its larger resource base, the Soviet Union grew in the late 1970s to be the largest oil producer in the world. Like the United States, the Soviet Union has large reserves of natural gas, coal, and uranium. Presumably from their resource positions alone, both countries would favor high energy prices.

If the Soviet Union feels that high world oil prices would slow down the industrial advance of Japan and West Germany, then that too would no doubt encourage Moscow to support such a price regime. It has lost one war with Japan in the twentieth century and has fought two bloody and costly wars with Germany. Surely the memories of such events color the attitudes of present Soviet officials about the economic growth of its former adversaries.

Large oil reserves make the Soviet Union one of a few nations that could expand oil exports to attack the cartel. Instead, the Soviet Union seems unable or unwilling to do much more than maintain current levels of exports to its customers in Eastern Europe and elsewhere. Moreover, in the 1970s the Soviet Union advised the countries of Eastern Europe to seek more oil imports from the Middle East. Based on present trends, the Soviet bloc (including the Soviet Union and Eastern Europe) may become a net oil importer in the 1980s, reversing its position as a net exporter which has been maintained through much of the postwar period.

For many years, the Soviet Union and Japan have been discussing the possibility of a joint venture to develop the Tyumen oil fields in Siberia. Japan had been interested in the Siberian venture as an opportunity to diversify its sources of oil, while the Soviet Union is lured by the possibility of material and monetary aid to speed the development of Siberia. But there are problems: although Siberian oil is of interest to Japan, neither Japan, China, nor the United States wishes to draw the Soviet Union eastward to the Pacific. For Japan, prior agreement with the United States would be an essential prerequisite to any such cooperation with the Soviet Union. Negotiations about the project seemed to stall in late 1973 when the United States indicated its unwillingness to provide financial support. Moreover, the Soviet Union may have no burning desire to help Japan out of its energy problems.

The Siberian venture is a particular example of the Soviet Union's underdeveloped potential as an oil exporter. Whatever the exact reasons in the case of Siberia, the general problems are political as well as technical, involving relationships with other strategic powers as well as with Japan and Western Europe. Whether by design or by the logic of parallel (if competing) interests, the Soviet Union in the 1970s seems to have followed a policy of de facto support for high oil prices.

While Japan has been frustrated in its negotiations with the Soviet Union for joint development of Siberian oil, it has been able to turn to China for an equivalent deal. Under the Sino-Japanese agreement signed in 1978, Japan will deliver industrial products to China in exchange for Chinese coal and oil. Although the amount of oil involved in the original agreement was not large in relation to total Japanese oil needs, improved Sino-Japanese relations through 1978 brought with them the expectation that oil imports from China may exceed 10 percent of Japan's oil needs by the late 1980s.[4]

China's oil production in 1977 was an estimated 1.8 million barrels daily.[5] In 1977 the U.S. Bureau of Mines projected an output of 4 million barrels per day (bbl/d) for China in 1987.[6] These figures are far below the 8 million bbl/d for the United States, 11 million bbl/d for the Soviet Union, or 10 million bbl/d for Saudi Arabia in 1977.[7] Nevertheless, China has decided to deliver a share of its oil production to foreign countries. The policy to develop oil production for export is driven by China's need for foreign technical and material assistance to support its ambitious plans for modernization. With the current high oil prices, oil promises to be one of China's key exports over the next decade or two.

China's oil reserves by the best recent foreign estimates may exceed those of the United States but are not as abundant as those of the Soviet Union.[8] China's oil industry in the 1970s, however, begins from a much smaller base. Thus, although expansion of output both for domestic consumption and export is expected to proceed quickly through the 1980s, the amounts of exports involved are not likely to prove upsetting to cartel price maintenance. Projected exports to Japan of one million barrels per day in 1990 represent, for example, only about 3 percent of OPEC's output in the 1970s. Moreover, Chinese oil—at least the Daqing (Taching) crude offered to Japan—has a high wax content and is difficult and expensive to refine.

Although China's oil exports are sold for a good price and the volumes involved even in the projections are not that large (smaller, for example, than the difference between Kuwait's installed production capacity and actual production in 1977) the political implications of the Sino-Japanese oil link are enormous. Political rapprochement and the treaty of peace and friendship signed by the two countries in August 1978 provided assurances of long-term political security that are necessary if the oil trade is to develop. While both Japan and China gain from their bilateral trade, the Soviet Union is visibly upset by the developing strength and unity of the strategic and industrial powers to its east. With its new source of oil in China, Japan has, for the time being, closed off any possibility of sharing in the development of Siberian oil fields. Negotiations between Japan and China over oil seem to have been linked to U.S.-Chinese understandings as well; in late 1978, for example, U.S. Energy Secretary James Schlesinger was in China at the same time that Chinese Vice-Premier Deng Xiaoping was in Tokyo discussing oil exports to Japan.

In the late 1970s, the United States seemed most concerned about the industrial challenge of Japan and West Germany. The Soviet Union, which is not a major trading nation, would presumably be more concerned about a possible military challenge in the future. If such concerns are expressed in oil policies, both of the two superpowers would be expected to follow policies to support high oil prices and even to restrict supplies to Japan and West Germany. China, with less of an ability to control world oil flows, nevertheless receives essential aid in its development from oil export revenues, which are dependent on the high price maintained by the cartel. In the context of Japan's dependence on foreign oil for about three-quarters of its total energy needs, imports from China provide some security through diversification, but do not relieve the pressure on Japan to restrain its future energy consumption. In sum, all three strategic continental powers have reasons to be happy with high oil prices, and neither the Soviet Union nor China is following policies that weaken the new high prices. This does not, of course, mean that the Soviet Union and the United States are in agreement about which of them should have the greatest influence in controlling oil supplies to Western Europe and Japan. Soviet attempts to upset the U.S.-dominated cartel, however, will be more likely to lead, through political instability in oil-exporting countries, to higher rather than lower international oil prices.

THE THIRD WORLD IN THE NEW WORLD ORDER

One recurrent theme in discussions about less developed countries in the 1970s has been that they may or ought to take OPEC's example and push for higher prices for their primary product exports. Fears of and hopes for such an occurrence are most often seen in terms of the world view of conventional wisdom, in which a deep political gulf separates the developed countries (of two ideologies) from the less developed, poor nations. Such a world view is supported by moralizers (who would have the rich be good to the poor), by radicals (who would have the poor rise up to smite the rich), and by the rich nations and their agents in power throughout the world (who are more than happy to hide their control behind a facade of various nationalisms).

The specter of Third World countries rising up to demand just prices from the industrialized countries has both supported and fed on the conventional, confused notion that the OPEC nations run their own cartel against the interests of all the industrialized nations, including the United States. A good example of popular mythology incorporating such confusions is given in a 1976 report by members of Congress who had been involved in multilateral negotiations with less developed countries.

> The growing frustration felt by the developing countries over their inability to receive a hearing from the advanced nations made them increasingly more radical on international issues. . . . Furthermore, this attitudinal change was given economic–political power by the energy crisis. Suddenly a group of developing nations had a monopoly on the marginal supplies of a key resource. When the industrial nations realized they were dependent on the OPEC nations for oil to fuel their economies, they also recognized more clearly that developing nations played an important role in other commodities. [9]

The world view behind such confusion supposes unity among the developed, industrialized nations, on the one hand, against the less developed primary product exporters on the other. An approximation to such a world order was only possible for several decades after World War II, when the United States with its preeminent economic power was able to organize most nations in the world into one vast multilateral system. Prior to World War II, the significant political divisions separated the British Empire (rich and poor nations together) from the French, Portuguese, or Belgian empires.

With widening cracks in Western unity and the continued decline of
the United States from its postwar position as preeminent economic
power, a retreat to the pre-World War II order of predominantly
vertical ties between poor and rich nations in various trade and currency blocs is likely to overtake the current fascination with the
poor nations in opposition to the rich.

The conventional wisdom of poor against rich has been insti-
tutionalized in the United Nations Conference on Trade and Development, a U.N.-sponsored series of international conferences in
which cartel control over some 18 different primary commodities in
world trade (including, for example, iron ore, bananas, vegetable
oil, and copper) has been publicly discussed. Although nations have
been represented in the meetings, multinational companies have
been active behind the scenes. The possibility of control by OPEC
of oil prices, as well as control by other groups of countries of the
prices of their different commodity exports, has always been dom-
inated by the role of the companies in organizing international trade.
But behind the companies stand the home countries, of which the
United States and, to a lesser extent, Great Britain, are the most
prominent in the 1970s.

As a continental and strategic power, the United States has
control of resources both within its borders as well as in other
countries through companies and through diplomatic and military
influence around the world. In the pattern of an aging empire, the
United States is likely to support cartel and producer agreements in
an attempt to aid client governments and U.S. companies at the expense of the importing nations. In the 1920s and 1930s, Great
Britain worked for cartels in rubber, tin, and oil. In the 1970s the
U.S. empire has produced cartels or suspected cartels in oil,
aluminum, and uranium.

Other industrial nations needing imports of raw materials
have understandably fought the cartels and have fought for influence
in the governments of resource-wealthy Third World countries.
Control over resources in Third World countries in the 1970s is
usually indirect; control is by proxy, through client governments,
rather than direct, through a colonial administration. Depending
on the legitimacy of the host country's government, control may be
more or less exact. In a country such as Australia, the scope for
outside manipulation may be small; in a military dictatorship with
one or two key generals, foreign manipulation may be personal and
exact.

During the 1950s and 1960s, the United States was able to operate in the Third World in most situations with the tacit or explicit
approval of other noncommunist industrial nations; the U.S. government and pro-U.S. factions in the governments of Third World nations,

such as the Philippines and Venezuela, for example, worried only about the communist faction. This simplified the task of control; since the Soviet Union was not a major trading nation, most nations with influential business elites were forced sooner or later, through domestic political developments, into a fairly high degree of cooperation with the United States.

During the late 1970s, however, and increasingly in the 1980s, several industrial noncommunist countries have been and will be jockeying for position in the resource-rich nations of the Third World. Important countries in Southeast Asia (Malaysia, Indonesia, and Thailand) and in Latin America (Brazil, Venezuela, Chile, and others) are likely to be the focus for proxy infighting by different factions representing the interests of Japan, West Germany, and the United States. The oil-producing nations of the Persian Gulf and of Africa will, of course, be major areas for competition.

In the 1970s the political situations in the oil-exporting nations, in Latin America, and in Southeast Asia in most cases seem relatively stable by comparison with Africa, which appears to be the biggest source of conflict for the 1980s. At the end of the nineteenth century, Africa was the last continent to be colonized; in the 1970s Africa has the least stable political conditions and offers the greatest opportunities for subversion and manipulation by industrial nations. Throughout Africa European nations have taken active roles in recent political and military struggles. South Africa poses a special problem with its mineral wealth (including uranium) and its abhorrent policy of apartheid. With Western unity breaking down in the 1970s, the opportunities for South Africa to find diplomatic and economic support are vastly improved. At the same time, the various factions for black rule in South Africa have become the focus for intense intrigue.

With West Germany and Japan pushing toward economic parity with the United States, it is not reasonable that the United States should bear the total cost of military and diplomatic intervention around the world without trying to make such intervention work for U.S. economic interests at the expense of Japan and West Germany. Similarly, Japan and West Germany will be led to intervene to protect their economic interests in key Third World governments. The intervention may take place initially on the level of economic aid, diplomatic effort, and so forth. The funding of political parties, payments to rebel groups, and attempts at conspiracy are likely to follow. Although it is unlikely that Third World countries will be officially recolonized, the pattern of control sought by the foreign industrial powers will be close and certain; the opportunities for intrigue with three or more competing foreign industrial powers present too much of a threat to loose or "democratic" control through

negotiated treaties with popular governments. Military dictator-
ships are neater and more certain. Economic competition between
the industrial powers is likely to lead to more repressive governments in the Third World.

DOMESTIC POLITICS AND INTERNATIONAL
ECONOMIC STRUGGLE

During the 1970s, the United States, West Germany, and Japan
have struggled continuously over various aspects of their international economic relations. Disagreements over trade and current-
account balances beginning in the late 1960s marked the arrival of
Japan and West Germany as industrial powers to be reckoned with.
In order to rebuild its trade surplus, the United States in 1971 uni-
laterally upset the system of multilateral agreement on fixed exchange rates which had been a central element of postwar economic
cooperation. Politically motivated manipulation of oil prices in
1973 further upset relations among the noncommunist industrial
powers; higher prices clearly benefited the United States at the expense of West Germany and Japan. West Germany and Japan responded with aggressive export drives that soon brought them record
trade and current-account surpluses despite larger oil-import bills.
Continued struggle between the major noncommunist industrial
powers over access to energy and other resources and over other
international economic issues seems certain to continue into the
future.

With the prominent involvement of governments in international economic affairs, which is a central feature of all these conflicts, domestic political processes will come to be more and more
involved with international economic issues. Such a development
brings risks for the maintenance of good relations between the various countries. Although they often disagree, the present leaders of
the United States, West Germany, and Japan are still inclined to
cooperate. Any serious deterioration in relations between the three
would be presaged by the advent of new groups of more narrowly
nationalistic leaders in one or more of the countries. Racist and
chauvinistic passions may be difficult to control under the constant
irritation of economic squabbles. Further serious deterioration of
relations among the noncommunist industrial powers is a dangerous
risk with the present international economic disorder.

NOTES

1. International Monetary Fund, International Financial Statistics, 32, 5 (Washington, D.C.: IMF, May 1979), pp. 390-91.

2. U.S. Department of Commerce, Bureau of the Census, Statistical Abstract of the United States, 1976 (Washington, D.C.: Government Printing Office, 1976), p. 881; International Monetary Fund, International Financial Statistics, 30, 11 (Washington, D.C.: IMF, November 1977), pp. 148-51, 204-7, 368-71.

3. Carroll L. Wilson, "A Plan for Energy Independence," in The World Economic Crisis, ed. William P. Bundy (New York: Norton, 1975), pp. 67-68.

4. George Lauriat, "Asia's Rapidly Changing Role in the Oil World," Far Eastern Economic Review, January 26, 1978, p. 38.

5. Melinda Liu, "Sobering Thoughts in the Oil Rush," Far Eastern Economic Review, November 3, 1978, p. 45.

6. K. P. Wang and staff, Bureau of Mines, U.S. Department of the Interior, Far East and South Asia (Washington, D.C.: Government Printing Office, 1977), p. 25.

7. U.S. Department of the Interior, Bureau of Mines, Mineral Commodity Summaries 1978 (Washington, D.C.: Government Printing Office, 1978), p. 123.

8. Liu, p. 45.

9. U.S. Congress, Senate, Committee on Foreign Relations et al., Report by Congressional Advisors to UNCTAD IV, 94th Cong. 2d sess., July 21, 1976, p. 1.

ABOUT THE AUTHOR

DR. DAVID GISSELQUIST is a Fellow on the staff of the Center for International Policy in Washington, D.C. This book grew out of work at the Center (1977-78) dealing with various aspects of international debt and trade deficits.

In addition to his work at the Center for International Policy, Dr. Gisselquist teaches economics—including the economics of energy—at the University of Maryland, Baltimore County. The author has also taught at the University of Massachusetts at Amherst, Thammasat University in Thailand (with the Rockefeller Foundation), and Chittagong University in Bangladesh (with the Ford Foundation). He received his PhD in economics from Yale University in 1976.

About the Author

Jeremy Kourdi is an internationally experienced executive coach, consultant and writer. He is Director of Kourdi Associates, a UK-based coaching and development business that helps leaders navigate and shape the future, and he is also a former Senior Vice President with *The Economist*. He provides experience and in-depth expertise in the fields of executive coaching and development, digital transformation, business strategy, leadership, and future thinking. Jeremy's background includes leadership, coaching, writing, consultancy and facilitation expertise gained with international brands, professional institutions and business schools. As well as being a qualified and supervized executive coach (qualified with Henley Business School) he also has an MA in International Relations and is the author/co-author of 27 books, translated into 17 languages.

During his career he has worked with a wide range of organizations including: Aramco, Deutsche Bank, The Economist Group, HSBC, Novartis, Pearson, Saudi British Bank, Tetra Pak, Zurich, IMD and London Business School. He has also interviewed Heads of Government and leading figures from business, as well as chairing conferences and government roundtables. Jeremy's work focuses on four broad areas: coaching, consultancy, digital transformation and content creation.

Jeremy lives in Surrey, south of London, and works with market-leading businesses and executives worldwide.

E: JK@Kourdi.com   T: +44 (0)7905 609590

Would you like your people to read this book?

If you would like to discuss how you could bring these ideas to your team, we would love to hear from you. Our titles are available at competitive discounts when purchased in bulk across both physical and digital formats. We can offer bespoke editions featuring corporate logos, customized covers, or letters from company directors in the front matter can also be created in line with your special requirements.

We work closely with leading experts and organizations to bring forward-thinking ideas to a global audience. Our books are designed to help you be more successful in work and life.

For further information, or to request a catalogue, please contact: **business@johnmurrays.co.uk**
sales-US@nicholasbrealey.com (North America only)

Nicholas Brealey Publishing is an imprint of John Murray Press.